JOHN POWELL, S.J.

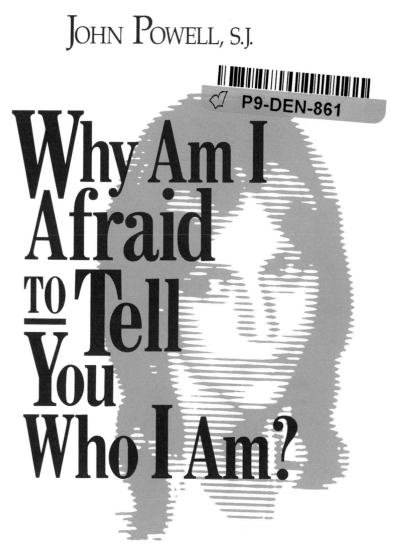

Why Am I Afraid TO Tell You Who I Am?

Insights into Personal Growth

TABOR®
PUBLISHING
Allen, Texas

Book Design: Chris Schechner Graphic Design

Cover Design: Debbie Allen

Calligraphy: Sue Bohlin, Bob Niles, Faith Scarborough,
    Chris Schechner

Photo Credits:
    C. David Edmonson: Pages 6, 23, 26, 31, 37, 44, 49, 56, 67, 74, 80, 118
    Jean-Claude Lejeune: Pages 10, 15, 20, 62, 92, 99, 104, 110, 139, 154

Send all inquiries to:
Tabor Publishing
200 Bethany Drive
Allen, Texas 75002

Library of Congress Catalog Number 70-113274

Printed in the United States of America

ISBN 1-55924-279-5

    3 4 5   94 93

Contents

1

Understanding the Human Condition

"How beautiful, how grand and liberating this experience is, when people learn to help each other. It is impossible to overemphasize the immense need humans have to be really listened to, to be taken seriously, to be understood.

"Modern psychology has brought it very much to our attention. At the very heart of all psychotherapy is this type of relationship in which one can tell everything, just as a little child will tell all to his mother.

"No one can develop freely in this world and find a full life without feeling understood by at least one person. . . .

"He who would see himself clearly must open up to a confidant freely chosen and worthy of such trust.

"Listen to all the conversations of our world, between nations as well as those between couples. They are for the most part dialogues of the deaf."

—Dr. Paul Tournier, M.D.
Swiss psychiatrist and author

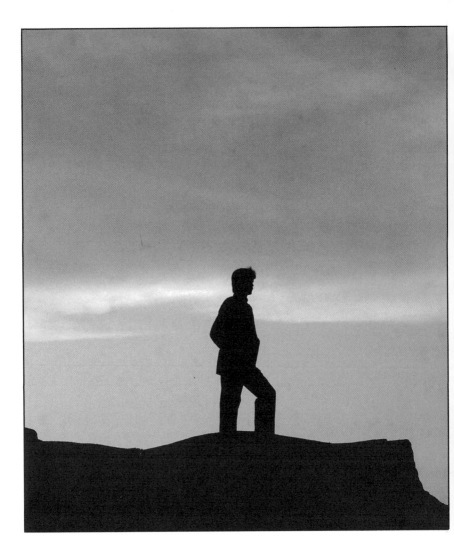

Then the Lord God said, "It is not good for man to be alone." *Genesis* 2:18

Our word *communication* refers to a process by which someone or something is made common, that is, it is shared. If you tell me a secret, then you and I possess the knowledge of your secret in common, and you have communicated it to me.

But you have much more to communicate to me, if you wish to, than merely one of your secrets. You can tell me who you are, just as I can tell you who I am.

THE "REAL" PERSON

In our society today, we have placed a great stress on being authentic. We have talked about placing masks over the face of our "real" selves, and of playing roles that disguise our true and real selves. The implication is that somewhere, inside you and inside me, lurk our real selves.

Supposedly, this real self is a static and formed reality. There are moments when this real self of mine shines out of me, and there are other moments when I feel compelled to camouflage my real self.

There is perhaps some justification for this manner of speaking, but I think that it can be more misleading than helpful. There is no fixed, true, and real person inside you or me, precisely because *being a person* necessarily implies *becoming a person, being in process.* If I am anything as a person, it is what I

> think
> judge
> feel
> value
> honor
> esteem
> love
> hate
> fear
> desire
> hope for
> believe in
> and
> am committed to.

These are the things that define my person, and they are constantly in process, in the process of change. Unless my mind and heart are hopelessly barricaded, all these things that define me as a person are forever changing.

My person is not a little hard core inside of me, a little fully formed statue that is real and authentic, permanent and fixed. My person rather implies a dynamic process. In other words, if you knew me yesterday, please do not think that I am the same person that you are meeting today.

I have experienced more of life, I have encountered new depths in those I love, I have suffered and prayed, and I am different.

Please do not give me a "batting average," fixed and irrevocable, because I am "in there" constantly, taking my swings at the opportunities of daily living. Approach me, then, with a sense of wonder, study my face and hands and voice for the signs of change; for it is certain that I have changed. But even if you do recognize this, I may be somewhat afraid to tell you who I am.

THE HUMAN CONDITION

Consider the following conversation:

Author: "I am writing a book, to be called *Why Am I Afraid to Tell You Who I Am?*"

Other: "Do you want an answer to your question?"

If I expose my nakedness
as a person
    to you,
do not make me feel shame.

Author: "That is the purpose of the book, to answer the question."

Other: "But do you want *my answer?*"

Author: "Yes, of course I do."

Other: "I am afraid to tell you who I am, because if I tell you who I am, you may not like who I am, and it's all that I have."

This short excerpt was taken from an actual conversation, unrehearsed and from life as it really is. It reflects something of the imprisoning fears and self-doubt which cripple most of us and keep us from forward movement on the road to maturity, happiness, and true love.

In a previous effort, entitled *Why Am I Afraid to Love?* (Tabor Publishing, 1967), I have tried to describe something of the human scars and pains that block the way to true love. They are the same scars, the same inner fears and pains, that block the way to true self-communication, on which love is built. Since that other publication, to which this is intended to be a sequel, is still available from Tabor Publishing, there is no need here to review the psychological dilemmas and distress that are a part of the human condition.

Nevertheless, as a progression from that earlier work, I do want to describe here something of how these scars, as well as the defenses that we use to protect ourselves from further vulnerability, tend to form patterns of action and reaction. These patterns eventually become so self-deceptive that we forfeit all sense of identity and integrity. We act out "roles," wear "masks," and play "games."

None of us wants to be a fraud or to live a lie; none of us wants to be a sham, a phony. But the fears that we experience and the risks that honest self-communication would involve seem so intense to us that seeking refuge in our roles, masks, and games becomes an almost natural reflex action.

After a while, it may even be quite difficult for us to distinguish between what we really are, at any given moment in our development as persons, and what we pose as being. It is such a universally human problem that we might justifiably call it "the human condition."

It is, at least, the condition in which most of us find ourselves and the point of our departure toward growth, integrity, and love.

TRANSACTIONAL ANALYSIS

The well-known California psychiatrist Dr. Eric Berne, in his best-selling book *The Games People Play*, speaks of "transactional analysis," by which he means an analysis of the social transaction when two people meet in a given situation. In such a situation, there is the "transactional stimulus" (for example, a sick child asking for a glass of water) and the "transactional response" (the mother bringing it). Transactional analysis attempts to diagnose the so-called "ego states" of the interacting persons (the stimulator and the respondent) at the time of the transaction. The supposition of transactional analysis is that, in various interactions, we may well be acting in a different role or ego state.

These ego states can be divided into three categories: the *Parent* (a collection of all the messages stored in us from infancy and child-hood), the *Adult* (the real me, capable of thinking my own thoughts and making my own decisions), and the *Child* (a storehouse of all the emotional responses of my life: the fears, angers, guilt complexes, and also the joys). None of us remains permanently fixed in any of these ego states, but we may fluctuate from one to another, depending on the situation at hand and our needs of the moment.

For example, the man who can at times function as a Parent to his child, or as an Adult to his wife or business associates, is also capable of assuming (either consciously or unconsciously) the ego state of a Child. While getting ready to escort his wife to the theater, where he will most probably assume the ego state of a Parent or an Adult, he may say impetuously to his wife, "Mama, will you please find my cuff links for me?" The Child (in this case, impatience and frustration) that is in him is suddenly activated because of his need of the moment. Of course, he may quickly revert to one of the other ego states, depending on his physical or emotional needs.

It may also happen that the respondent in the example given is inclined to avoid any responsibilities, and the Child in the wife may come to the surface. "Gee whiz, Daddy, if you can't find them, I'm sure that I certainly can't." The "vector line" is strictly horizontal in this transaction: Child is relating to Child. Emotions are in control in both persons.

HOW WE ARE "PROGRAMMED" TO CHOOSE EGO STATES

Clinical experimentation, applying these theories, has operated on the assumption that all of us are capable of these various ego states, and that we have been programmed by our individual, psychological histories to react as Parent, Adult, or Child, in given life situations. This "programming" is a result of the composite of previous influences in our lives (social programming) and our reaction to them (individual programming). The stimuli of these previous influences and reactions are recorded indelibly inside us.

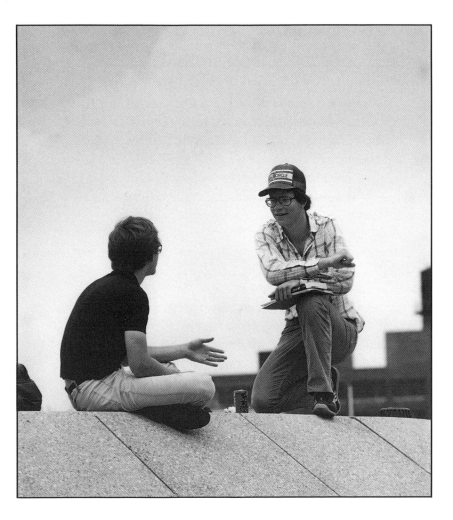

I can help you to accept and
open yourself
mostly by accepting and
revealing myself to you.

As human organisms we carry within ourselves something like a portable tape recorder, which is always playing softly but insistently inside us. On the tape of this recorder there plays the message of Mother or Father (or other). Mother may still be saying: "Nothing is too good for my little Darling. I'll do the dishes and make the beds. You just run along and play, Honey." If the reaction of "Honey" was to accept this message and act out the role of the perpetual child, you may see her (supposed by now to be an adult) running right by you someday, on her way to play. She is still expecting others to do everything for her, and is unwilling to take any responsibility. She is reassured by her parent-tapes.

Or Daddy's thunder may be the parent-message on the tape recorder: "You're no damned good, you Louse!" If the child in this case has reacted in a docile manner, he is likely to be sullen and discouraged when he passes you. He will probably be mumbling to himself: "I'm no damned good . . . I'm no damned good!"

Social programming and individual programming tend to crystallize in patterns of action and reaction. These patterns can often be predicted in most of us with high accuracy. Depending on our habits and habitual reactions, we tend to play the same roles, the same "games." And the "game" always follows the "program." If you want to understand the game correctly, it helps to know the program.

PROGRAMMING: WHO WILL DOMINATE IN THE PSYCHODRAMA?

Inside each of us, there is a tape recorder that plays the sound track of a psychodrama that is continually being enacted. On the stage is the Parent, the Child, and the Adult. The Mother or Father is delivering a message to the Child. The Child is reacting emotionally to the message. When the Adult hears the message and sees the reaction of the Child, he or she has to step in and corroborate or deny the message. The Adult has to be assertive, because if not, the whole future of the person involved will be nothing more than a living out of the programming of the past. The Parent and/or Child will dominate such a life.

For example, if the Parent is saying, "You'll never amount to anything," the Adult has to step in and deny this message. "Stop telling this child that he or she is no good!" Only when the message is expunged by the intervention of the Adult can the person act and feel worthwhile.The balance can and has to be tipped. Life has to be more than simply a living out of the program-ming of the past, and it can be if the Adult in us will intervene.

When we speak or act, sometimes the Parent in us is in control, is speaking (the parental message is indelible and always operative). Sometimes the Child in us takes over. Our emotions begin to make our decisions for us. Sometimes we get plugged into the Adult. There are times, too, when the Parent in us interrupts the Child, as, for example: "It is such a nice day outside and I would like to go out and play (Child), but you can't always be doing what you want to (Parent)." At this point the intervening Adult may be assertive and decide: "But I need some fresh air and I need it now, so I'm going out."

There is in each of us not only a variety of ego states but also an *acculturated self* and a *deliberated self*. This distinction is essentially the same as the distinction between the programmed self and the intervening Adult self. The culture or subculture in which we live is one of the sources of our programming. It sets us up to react to certain situations in certain ways. When we oblige others with the expected reactions, or when we fall into patterns that have been pretty much determined by our past, it is the *acculturated* self that is acting. As a person becomes more and more adult (mature) the *deliberated* self, which acts out of personal integration and conviction, takes over. The fully human being is gradually extricated from his or her programming and turns from being a "reactor" to being an "actor." The person becomes "his own man" or "her own woman."

RESORTING TO GAMES

"Games" in this context are not really fun. They are our patterned reactions to life situations, programmed for us somewhere back in our personal, psychological history. Sometimes these games are extremely grim affairs, because everyone is playing to win—to win something. In order to achieve the honest communication of ourselves to others, to experience the reality of others, to become integrated and to grow, it helps very much to be aware of these patterned reactions—the games we play. If we become consciously aware of these games, we may give them up.

These games are almost always little maneuvers on our part, which we employ to avoid self-realization and self-communication. They are little shields, which we carry in front of us as we enter the battle of life. They are designed to protect us from being hurt and to help us win some little trophy for our egos. Eric Berne calls these little gains "strokes," little victories or successes that bring us protection or recognition. The games are various because psychological histories and programming are always unique. The games also vary because there are three ego states in which we may choose to cast ourselves, depending on the needs of the moment and the life situation.

"BUT IF I TELL YOU
WHO I AM,
YOU MAY NOT LIKE
WHO I AM,
AND IT IS ALL
THAT I HAVE."

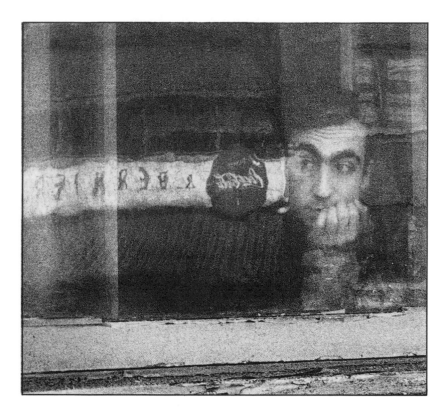

The one thing that all of these games have in common is this: They defeat self-knowledge and destroy all possibility of honest self-communication with others. The price of victory is costly; there is little chance for game players to experience true interpersonal relationships, which alone can put them on the path to human growth and the fullness of human life.

Most of us play games with others in our habitual behavior. We set others up to react to us in the way that we want them to react. For example, we may not ever grow into authentic persons because we have settled for being children, inadequate and in need. We send out our "pity signals" in the sound of our voices and in the expressions on our faces. We attempt to condition others to react very gently to us. We sound and look as helpless as any child; most people are obliging enough to follow our stage directions.

Others of us, who are messianic in our assumed role, insist on wanting to save others at all times. We want to be "the helper" and to make everyone else to whom we relate "the helped." Sometimes the perpetual child marries the messiah, and they make a lifelong game of it together. Since these two games mesh, things will go very well, and neither of them will ever have to grow up. However, if one of them decides to "grow up," there will be sparks of conflict.

It is our fears and insecurity that prompt us to assume various ego states and play various games. However, if we try to be in honest touch with our emotions and to report them truthfully, the patterns of "pity signals" or "messianic mystique" will become obvious even to us. And that is the moment of change.

The perpetual child would find that she never relates well to others except when she is bringing her problems and helplessness to them. The self-styled savior would discover that he never relates well to others unless the other is troubled and helpless . . . and needing him. Being honest with one's self in this way is no easy matter, because it involves letting one's repressed emotions rise to recognition for what they really are. It also demands reporting these emotions to others, as we shall see later.

It is doubtful that there is anyone who does not play these or other games. Therefore, if I really want to "see it like it is . . . and tell it like it is," I must ask myself some difficult questions about the patterns of action and reaction that emerge in my conduct, and I must ask myself what these patterns reveal to me about myself.

Do I subconsciously develop problems in order to get attention? Do I insist on relegating all those with whom I relate to the category of "those who need my help"? Do I present myself as delicate in

I can only know
that much
of myself
which I have had
the courage to
confide to you.

order to insure gentle treatment from others? Am I using other people as conquests to provide a transfusion of life for my limping ego? Am I seeking to impress others with my self-sufficiency, precisely because I doubt my adequacy as a person? Hard and probing questions, aren't they?

The final section of this book is a partial listing of some of the more common roles that people assume for either permanent or occasional use. It could be called a "catalog of games and roles." This catalog, however, is not intended at all to be the "entertainment" section. All of us experience the "human condition" of fear and hiding. We all know something of what was meant by: "But if I tell you who I am, you may not like who I am, and it is all that I have."

What you and I really need is to come to a moment of truth and to develop a habit of truth with ourselves. We have to ask ourselves in the quiet, personal privacy of our own minds and hearts: What games do I play? What is it that I am trying to hide? What is it that I hope to win?

My willingness to be honest with myself and these questions will be the decisive factor and the essential condition for growth as a person.

Growing people are self-renewing, —as new as each new day. Study their faces and hands and voices for signs of change, for it is certain that they have changed.

2

Growing as a Person

I n these pages there are frequent references to "growth as a person," and much will be said about the necessity of self-communication and interpersonal encounter as a means to this growth. It is both intriguing and difficult to try to describe what this "growth" implies. It is impossible to cite an example of the full-grown person because each of us has to grow into his or her own person, not become "like" anyone else.

What kind of a person are we trying to become? Carl Rogers calls this person "the fully functioning person" *(Psychotherapy: Theory, Research, and Practice*, 1963) and certainly, since becoming a person is a lifelong, dynamic process, growth will have to be defined largely in terms of functions. The late Abraham Maslow, the famous psychologist from Brandeis University, calls this person "the self-actualizing person," and "the fully human person."

INTERIORITY AND EXTERIORITY

The fully human person preserves a balance between "interiority" and "exteriority." Both the extreme introvert and the extreme extrovert are off balance. Introverts are almost exclusively concerned with themselves; they become the center of gravity in their own universe. Because of their preoccupation with self, introverts are distracted from the vast world outside. Extreme extroverts, on the other hand, pour themselves out, move from one external distraction to another. Their lives are not very reflective, and consequently they experience little interior deepening. As Socrates said, "The unreflected life isn't worth living." Thus the first condition of growth is balance: a balance of interiority and exteriority.

"Interiority" implies exploration and experience of self. People who have explored and experienced themselves are aware of the vitality of their senses, emotions, mind, and will. They are neither a stranger to, nor afraid of, the activities of their body and emotions. Their senses bring them both beauty and pain, and they refuse neither. They are capable of the whole gamut of human emotions: from grief to tenderness. Their minds are alive and searching; their wills reach out for an ever greater possession of all that is good and at the same time savor that which is already in their possession. They have listened to

themselves, and they know that nothing which they hear is evil or frightening.

"Interiority" implies self-acceptance. The desired interiority means that fully functioning, self-actualizing, fully human people not only are aware of physical, psychological, and spiritual hungers and activities, but also accept them as good. Such people are "at home" with their bodies, their tender as well as hostile emotions, their impulses, thoughts, and desires.

Not only are fully human people "at home" with what they have already experienced within themselves, but they are open to new sensations, new and deeper emotional reactions, changing thoughts and desires. They accept their inner condition as forever changing, since growth always involves change. Their ultimate destiny as human beings, that is, what they will become at the end of their lives, is delightfully unknown. No human growth patterns can be prestructured for all. These people do not ambition to turn out like anyone else, because they are themselves. Their potential selves, newly actualized every day by new experiences, cannot possibly be defined at any one stage of their growth.

Fully human people accept what they are, physically, emotionally, and intellectually. They know that what they are, as far as it is known to them, is good; they know that their potential selves are even greater. They are, however, realistic about their limitations; they do not dwell in dreams of what they *want* to be and spend the rest of their lives convincing themselves that they *are* these things. They have listened to, explored, and loved what they actually are. And each new day this experience of themselves will be as new as the day itself because they are forever changing, always new persons, revealed in a constantly changing, self-renovating personality. They trust their own abilities and resources, confident that they can adapt to and cope with all the challenges that their lives will present.

This kind of self-acceptance empowers people to live fully and confidently with all that goes on inside them. They are afraid of nothing that is or could be a part of themselves.

"Exteriority" implies an openness not only to the self within but to the environment from without. Fully human people are in deep and meaningful contact with the world outside of them. They listen not only to themselves but to the voices of their world. The breadth of their own individual experience is infinitely multiplied through a sensitive empathy with others. They suffer with the suffering, rejoice with the joyful. They are born again in every springtime, feel the impact of the great mysteries of life: birth, growth, love, suffering, death. Their hearts skip along with the "young lovers," and they know something of the

The greatest kindness
    I have to offer you
is always:
        THE TRUTH.

exhilaration that is in them. They also know the ghetto's philosophy of despair, the loneliness of suffering without relief. The bell never tolls without tolling in some strange way for them.

"Create in me, O God, a listening heart," the psalmist prays.

The opposite of this openness is a kind of "defensiveness." This defensiveness hears only what it wants to hear, according to its own preconceived structure and bias. It sees only what it wants to see. Defensive people cannot be growing people because their world is no bigger than themselves, and the circle of their horizons is tightly closed.

"Exteriority" reaches its peak in the ability to "give love freely." Dr. Karl Stern, a psychiatrist of deep insight, has said that the evolution of human growth is an evolution from an *absolute need to be loved* (infancy) toward *a full readiness to give love* (maturity), with all sorts of stages in between. Dr. Stern said: "In our primary state of union (at the beginning of our growth as persons) we are selfish, and I am, of course, not using the word in its usual moral connotation. The infantile self is still *id* (Freud's term for our drives and ambitions) without differentiation of *ego* (that which, in the Freudian system, adapts and harmonizes personal drives with reality); the *id* of the infantile self is all-engulfing without proper

awareness of its own borders. The acts of union of the mature personality are *self-less*."*

Fully human beings can go outside of themselves, can be committed to a cause; and they do this *freely*. Of course, fully human beings must be free. There are many philanthropists among us who give of their goods or their time addictively or compulsively. There seems to be some driving need that leaves them restless, some guilt or anxiety that becomes an obsessive ring in the nose, leading these people from one good deed to another. Fully human beings go out to others and to God, not by a kind of compulsive-obsessive neurosis, but actively and freely, and simply because they have chosen to do so.

The philosopher Martin Heidegger, in discussing the unions of love, points out two pitfalls that can stifle human growth: a complacent satisfaction that settles for that which already is, and, at the other extreme, a restless activity that goes from distraction to distraction in search of something beyond. The result, says Heidegger, is always self-estrangement. In love we must possess and savor that which is, and simultaneously reach out to possess (to love) the

*Institute of Man Symposium on *Neurosis and Personal Growth*, Duquesne University, Pittsburgh, Pa., November 18, 1966.

good more fully. This is the balance achieved by fully human beings. It is the balance between "what is" and "what is to come."

Fully human beings, in their love, do not identify themselves with what they love, as though these loved things were extensions of themselves. Gabriel Marcel, in his book *Being and Having*, laments that our civilization teaches us how to take possession of things, when it should rather initiate us in the art of letting go. There is neither freedom nor real life without an apprenticeship in dispossession.

Balanced "interiority" and "exteriority" is what is meant by integration of personality. Human nature, contrary to much that has been implied about it, is basically reasonable. Carl Rogers insists that this is his certain conclusion, based on twenty-five years of work in psychotherapy. A person is not a forest of irrational desires and impulses. If this were so, people would not want to be fully human. We are all of us capable of exaggeration. We can turn too much inward or outward. We can become slaves to our sense pleasures without reflection on our peace of soul or on our social need to love and to give to others. Or we can exaggerate by becoming prisoners of "intellect," alive only from the neck up.

When people live fully in all of their faculties, and harmonize all of their powers, human nature will prove constructive and trustworthy. In other words, as Rogers points out, when we function freely, our reactions may be trusted; they will be positive, forward moving, constructive. This is a great act of faith in human nature that too few of us ever make: If people are truly open to all that they are, and if they function freely and fully in all of their powers (senses, emotions, mind, and will), their behavior will harmonize all the data of their powers, and will be balanced and realistic. They will be on the path to growth, and that is our human destiny, not perfection but growth.

ACTING VS. REACTING

The fully human person is an actor, not a reactor. Sydney Harris, the syndicated columnist, tells the story of accompanying his friend to a newsstand. The friend greeted the newsman very courteously, but in return received gruff and discourteous service. Accepting the newspaper that was shoved rudely in his direction, the friend of Harris politely smiled and wished the newsman a nice weekend. As the two friends walked down the street, the columnist asked:

"Does he always treat you so rudely?"

"Yes, unfortunately he does."

"And are you always so polite and friendly to him?"

"Yes, I am."

"Why are you so nice to him when he is so unfriendly to you?"

"Because I don't want *him* to decide how *I'm* going to act."

The suggestion is that "fully human" people are "their own persons," that they do not bend to every wind which blows, that they are not at the mercy of all the pettiness, the meanness, the impatience and anger of others. Atmospheres do not transform them as much as they transform their atmospheres.

Most of us, unfortunately, feel like a floating boat at the mercy of the winds and waves. We have no ballast when the winds rage and the waves churn. We say things like: "He made me so mad." "You really get to me." "Her remark embarrassed me terribly." "This weather really depresses me." "This job really bores me." "The very sight of him saddens me."

Note that all these things are *doing something to me and to my emotions.* I have nothing to say about my anger, depression, sadness, and so on. And like everyone else we are content to blame others, circumstances, and bad luck. Fully human people, as Shakespeare puts it in *Julius Caesar*, know that "the fault, dear Brutus, is not with our

your slightest look
easily will unclose me
though i have closed myself as fingers,
you open always petal by petal
myself as spring opens
(touching skillfully, mysteriously)
her first rose

e.e. cummings

stars, but with ourselves." We must learn that we can rise above the dust of daily battle that chokes and blinds so many of us. This is precisely what is asked of us in the process of growth as a person.

There is nothing implied here that suggests *repression* of emotions or that denies the fullness of life in our senses and emotions. The suggestion is rather of *balance* and *integration* of emotions. In fully alive human beings, there can be no such thing as either deadening or unconditionally surrendering to the senses or emotions.

Fully alive people listen to, are attuned to their senses and emotions. However, surrendering to them would imply abdication of intellect and choice. These are the precise powers that make human beings more than brute animals, though a little less than the angels. We will say more of this reconciliation of senses, emotions, intellect, and will in the next chapter (see "Rule three").

3

Interpersonal Relationships

Harry Stack Sullivan, one of the more eminent psychiatrists of interpersonal relationships in our times, has propounded the theory that all personal growth, all personal damage and regression, as well as all personal healing and growth, come through our relationships with others. There is a persistent, if uninformed, suspicion in most of us that we can solve our own problems and be the masters of our own ships of life. The fact of the matter is that by ourselves we can only be consumed by our problems and suffer shipwreck. What I am, at any given moment in the process of my becoming a person, will be determined by my relationships with those who love me or refuse to love me, with those whom I love or refuse to love.

It is certain that a relationship will be *only as good as its communication.* If you and I can honestly tell each other who we are, that is, what we think, judge, feel, value, love, honor and esteem, hate, fear, desire, hope for, believe in, and are committed to, then and then only can each of us grow. Then and then alone can we be what we really are, say what we really think, tell what we really feel, express what we really love. This is the real meaning of authenticity as a person, that my exterior truly reflects my interior. It means I can be honest in the com-munication of my person to others. This I cannot do unless you help me. Unless you help me, I cannot grow, or be happy, or really come alive.

I have to be free and able to say my thoughts to you, to tell you about my judgments and values, to expose to you my fears and frustrations, to admit to you my failures and shames, to share my triumphs, before I can really be sure what it is that I am and can become. I must be able to tell you who I am before I can know who I am. And I must know who I am before I can act truly, that is, in accordance with my true self.

THE SUBJECT-OBJECT RELATIONSHIP VS. THE "ENCOUNTER"

In the language of existential psychology, "encounter" describes a special relationship between two persons. It implies that a commu-nion or communication of persons has been achieved. One existence is communicating to another existence, is sharing with another. Gabriel Marcel calls this kind of relationship an "ontological communion," a real fusion of two people. To illustrate what this means, Marcel explains that very often our emotions and sympathy do not spring to life at all when we encounter the suffering of others in our daily lives. Somehow, Marcel goes on, I just cannot respond to them; they are just "not there" for me. But if we should open a letter from a friend many miles away telling us of some great disaster or sickness, we are at once with that friend, suffering with him or her; we are together without any qualification.

In the words of Martin Buber, the Jewish philosopher of interpersonality, it is in the *encounter* that the other individual no longer is a person of impersonality, a "he" or "she," but becomes for my "I" a sensitized, correlative "Thou." (See Martin Buber, *I-Thou* [New York: Scribner, 1958].) The other person becomes, in some mysterious and almost undefinable way, a special being in my eyes, a part of my world, and a part of my self. Insofar as it is possible, I enter into the world of the other's reality and he or she enters into the world of my reality. There has been some kind of fusion, even though each of us always remains a distinct self. As e. e. cummings writes:

"One's not half two. It's two are halves of one."

My friend of encounter is no longer someone "out there somewhere" who serves my purposes, or who belongs to my club, or who works with me. Ours is no such subject-object relationship; we have experienced that mysterious but certain communion of togetherness. It is this that the existential psychologists call "encounter." And the stuff of which encounter is made is honest communication.

Where true encounter exists, and we are saying that it is absolutely essential for growth as a person, the concern of the persons in such an encounter is not so much with the problems and their solutions as with the communion, the sharing. I open myself and my world to you for your entry, and you open yourself and your world to me for me to enter. I have allowed you to experience me as a person, in all the fullness of my person, and I have experienced you in this way. And for this, I must tell you who I am and you must tell me the same about yourself. Communication is the only avenue to communion.

This is why psychologists such as Erich Fromm say that we cannot love anyone without loving everyone more. If I can communicate with you and you with me only on a "subject-object" level, we will probably both communicate with others, and even with God, on this same level. We will remain isolated subjects; others and God will remain merely "objects" in our world, but not experiences. Unless we have been opened up by such an encounter, we will have so-called friendships, and will perhaps retain a so-called religious faith (a kind of relationship with God), mostly because these are things that are somehow expected of us. These relationships with others will be social amenities and nothing more. There will be no personal meaning in them.

The world of people in subject-object relationships is a world of objects, things to be manipulated, to serve as distractions or sources of pleasure. The possessions of such people may be beautiful and expensive or common and cheap, but these people will be lonely. They will come to the end of life without ever having really lived. The dynamic process of personhood will become a static thing like debris floating on stagnant waters. When the process of personhood is stifled, all of life becomes a terrible bore. If the edges of reality for a humanly isolated person are sharp, life can be very painful. There will seem to be need for those artificially induced but short-lived stimuli called "kicks." These kicks are little attempts to run away from life, short "trips," in an effort to escape the inexorable intrusion of reality and the essential loneliness of the person without true friends.

Human life has its laws, one of which is: We must *use* things and *love* people. People whose whole lives are lived on the subject-object level

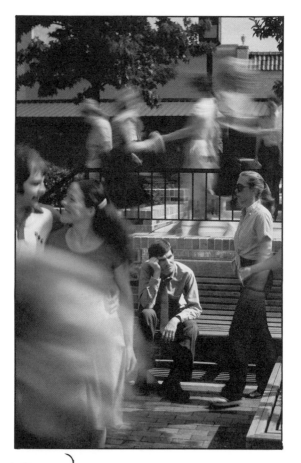

To refuse the invitation
to interpersonal encounter is
to be an isolated dot in the
center of a great circle
—a small island in a vast ocean.

find that they love things and use people. It is the death warrant for happiness and human fulfillment.

INTERPERSONAL ENCOUNTER AND THE FIVE LEVELS OF COMMUNICATION

Someone has aptly distinguished five levels of communication on which persons can relate to one another. Perhaps it will help our understanding of these levels to visualize a person locked inside of a prison. The prisoner in our example is a man, but he represents every human being. He is urged by an inner insistence to go out to others and yet afraid to do so. The five levels of communication, which will be described a little later, represent five degrees of willingness to go outside of the self, to communicate the self to others.

The man in the prison—and he is everyone— has been there for years, although ironically the grated iron doors are not locked. He can go out of his prison, but in his long detention he has learned to fear the possible dangers that he might encounter. He has come to feel some sort of safety and protection behind the walls of his prison, where he is a voluntary captive. The darkness of his prison shields him from a clear view of himself. He is not sure what he would look like in broad daylight. Above all, he is not sure how the world, which he sees from behind bars, and the people whom he sees moving about in that world, would receive him. He is fragmented by an almost desperate need for that world and for those people, and, at the same time, by an almost desperate fear of the risks of rejection he would be taking if he ended his isolation.

This prisoner is reminiscent of what Viktor Frankl writes, in his book *Man's Search for Meaning,* about his fellow prisoners in the Nazi concentration camp at Dachau. These prisoners yearned desperately for their freedom. Yet some of them had been held captive so long that when they were eventually released, they walked out into the sunlight, blinked nervously, and then silently walked back into the familiar darkness of the prison. They had been accustomed to this darkness for such a long time.

This is the visualized, if somewhat dramatic, dilemma that all of us experience at some time in our lives and in the process of becoming persons. Most of us make only a weak response to the invitation of encounter with others and our world because we feel uncomfortable in exposing our nakedness as persons. Some of us are willing only to pretend this exodus, while others somehow find in themselves the courage to go all the way out to freedom. There are various stages in between. These stages are described below, under the headings of the five levels of communication. The fifth level, to be considered first, represents the least willingness to communicate ourselves to others. The successive, descending levels indicate greater and greater success in the adventure.

Level Five: Cliché Conversation. This level represents the weakest response to the human dilemma and the lowest level of self-communication. In fact, there is no communication here at all, unless by accident. On this level, we talk in clichés, such as: "How are you?" "How is your family?" "Where have you been?" We say things like: "I like your dress very much." "I hope we can get together again real soon." "It's really good to see you." In fact, we really mean almost nothing of what we are asking or saying. If the other party were to begin answering our question "How are you?" in detail, we would be astounded. Usually and fortunately, the other party senses the superficiality and conventionality of our concern and question. People usually oblige by simply giving the standard answer, "Just fine, thank you."

This is the conversation, the noncommunication, of the cocktail party, the club meeting, the neighborhood laundromat, and so on. There is no sharing of persons at all. Everyone remains safely in the isolation of his or her pretense, sham, sophistication. The whole group seems to gather in order to be lonely together. It is well summarized in the lyrics of Paul Simon's "Sounds of Silence," used so effectively in the movie *The Graduate:*

"And in the naked night I saw
Ten thousand people, maybe more,
People talking without speaking,
People hearing without listening,
People writing songs that voices never shared.
No one dared
Disturb the sounds of silence."

Level Four: Reporting the Facts about Others. On this fourth level, we do not step very far outside the prison of our loneliness into real communication because we expose almost nothing of ourselves. We remain contented to tell others what so-and-so has said or done. We offer no personal, self-revelatory commentary on these facts. We simply report them. Just as most of us, at times, hide behind clichés, so we also seek shelter in gossip items, conversation pieces, and little narrations about others. We give nothing of ourselves and invite nothing from others in return.

Level Three: My Ideas and Judgments. On this level, there is some communication of my person. I am willing to take this step out of my solitary confinement. I will take the risk of telling you some of my ideas and reveal some of my judgments and decisions. My communication

Most people tend to overcompensate . . . .

People who are riddled with doubts tend to be dogmatists who are never wrong.

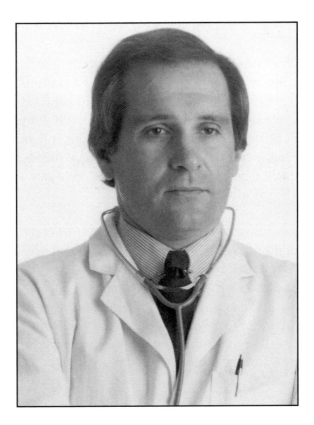

usually remains under a strict censorship, however. As I communicate with you, I will be watching you carefully. I want to test the temperature of the water before I leap in. I want to be sure that you will accept me with my ideas, judgments, and decisions. If you raise your eyebrow or narrow your eyes, if you yawn or look at your watch, I will probably retreat to safer ground. I will run for the cover of silence or change the subject of conversation. Or worse, I will start to say things I suspect that you want me to say. I will try to be whatever pleases you.

Someday, perhaps, when I develop the courage and the intensity of desire to grow as a person, I will spill all of the contents of my mind and heart before you. It will be my moment of truth. It may even be that I have already done so, but still you can know only a little about my person, unless I am willing to advance to the next level of self-communication.

Level Two: My Feelings (Emotions)—"Gut Level." It might not occur to many of us that, once we have revealed our ideas, judgments, and decisions, there is really much more of our persons to share. Actually, the things that most clearly differentiate and individuate me from others, that make the communication of my person a unique knowledge, are my *feelings* or *emotions.*

If I really want you to know who I am, I must tell you about my stomach (gut level) as well as my head. My ideas, judgments, and decisions are quite conventional. If I am a Republican or Democrat by persuasion, I have a lot of company. If I am for or against space exploration, there will be others who will support me in my conviction. But the *feelings* that lie under my ideas, judgments, and convictions are uniquely mine. No one supports a political party, or has a religious conviction, or is committed to a cause with my exact feelings of fervor or apathy. No one experiences my precise sense of frustration, labors under my fears, feels my passions. Nobody opposes war with my particular indignation or supports patriotism with my unique sense of loyalty.

It is these feelings, on this level of communication, that I must share with you if I am to tell you who I really am. To illustrate this, I would like to put in the left-hand column a judgment, and in the right-hand column some of the possible emotional reactions to this judgment. If I tell you only the contents of my mind, I will be withholding a great deal about myself, especially in those areas where I am uniquely personal, most individual, most deeply myself.

Judgment	*Some possible emotional reactions*
I think that you are intelligent.	. . . and I am jealous.
	. . . and I feel frustrated.
	. . . and I feel proud to be your friend.
	. . . and it makes me ill at ease with you.
	. . . and I feel suspicious of you.
	. . . and I feel inferior to you.
	. . . and I feel impelled to imitate or compete with you.
	. . . and I feel like running away from you.
	. . . and I feel the desire to humiliate you.

Most of us feel that others will not tolerate such emotional honesty in communication. We would rather defend our dishonesty on the grounds that it might hurt others. Having rationalized our phoniness into nobility, we settle for superficial relationships. This occurs not only in the case of casual acquaintances but even with members of our own families; it destroys authentic communion within marriages and families. Consequently, we ourselves do not grow, nor do we help anyone else to grow. Meanwhile we have to live with repressed emotions—a dangerous and self-destructive path to follow. Any relationship that is to have the nature of true personal encounter must be based on this honest, open, gut-level communication. The alternative is to remain in a prison of isolation, to endure inch-by-inch death as a person.

We will say more of this level of communication, after describing the first and deepest level of communication between persons.

Level One: Peak Communication. All deep and authentic friendships, and especially the union of those who are married, must be based on absolute openness and honesty. At times, gut-level communication will be most difficult, but it is at these precise times that it is most necessary. Among close friends or between partners in marriage there will come from time to time a complete emotional and personal communion.

In our human condition this can never be a permanent experience. There should and will be, however, moments when encounter attains perfect communication. At these times the two persons will feel an almost perfect and mutual empathy. I know that my own reactions are shared completely by my friend; my happiness or my grief is perfectly reduplicated in him or her. We are like two musical instruments playing exactly the same note, filled with and giving forth precisely the same sound. This is what is meant by level one, peak communication. (Cf. A. H. Maslow, *Religions, Values, and Peak Experiences,* 1964.)

"RULES" FOR GUT-LEVEL COMMUNICATION

If friendship and human love are to mature between any two persons, there must be absolute and honest mutual revelation. This kind of self-revelation can be achieved only through what we have called "gut-level" communication. There is no other way, and all the reasons that we adduce to rationalize our cover-ups and dishonesty must be seen as delusions. It would be much better for me to tell you how I really feel about you than to enter into the stickiness and discomfort of a phony relationship.

Dishonesty always has a way of coming back to haunt and trouble us. Even if I should have to tell you that I do not admire or love you emotionally, it would be much better than trying to deceive you and having to pay the ultimate price of all such deception, your greater hurt and mine. And you will have to tell me things, at times, that will be difficult for you to share. But really, you have no choice. If I want your friendship, I must be ready to accept you as you are. If either of us comes to the relationship without this determination of mutual honesty and openness, there can be no friendship, no growth. Rather, there can be only a subject-object kind of thing that is typified by adolescent bickering, pouting, jealousy, anger, and accusations.

The classic temptation in this matter, and it would seem to be the most destructive of all delusions in this area of human relations, is this: We are tempted to think that communication of an unfavorable emotional reaction will tend to be divisive. If I tell you that it bothers me when you do something you are accustomed to doing, I may be tempted to believe that it would be better not to mention it. Our relationship will be more peaceful. You wouldn't understand, anyway.

So I keep it inside myself, and each time you do your thing my stomach keeps score—2 . . . 3 . . . 4 . . . 5 . . . 6 . . . 7 . . . 8 . . . Then one day you do the same thing that you have always done and all hell breaks loose. All the while I was feeling annoyed, I was keeping it inside and somewhere, secretly, learning to hate you. My good thoughts were slowly turning to gall.

When it finally erupted in one great emotional avalanche, you didn't understand. You thought that this kind of reaction was totally uncalled for. The bonds of our love seemed fragile and about to break. And it all started when I thought: "I don't like what she [he] is doing, but it would be

To reveal myself
openly and honestly
takes the
rawest kind of courage.

better not to say anything. The relationship will be more peaceful." That was all a delusion, and I should have told you in the beginning. Now there has been an emotional divorce. Our relationship is strained or ruptured. And all because I wanted to keep the peace between us.

Rule one: Gut-level communication (emotional openness and honesty) must never imply a judgment of the other. I am simply not mature enough to enter into true friendship unless I realize that I cannot judge the intention or motivation of another. I must be humble and sane enough to bow before the complexity and mystery of a human being. If I judge you, I have only revealed my own immaturity and ineptness for friendship.

Emotional candor as such does not ever imply a judgment of you. In fact, it even abstains from any judgment of myself. For example, if I were to say to you, "I am ill at ease with you," I have been emotionally honest and at the same time have not implied in the least that it is your fault that I am ill at ease with you. Perhaps it is my own inferiority complex or my exaggerated concept of your intelligence. I am not saying it is anyone's fault, but simply giving a report of my emotional reaction to you at this time.

If I were to say to you that I feel angry or hurt by something you have done or said, I have not judged you. Perhaps it is my own self-love that has made me so sensitive, or my inclination to paranoia (a persecution complex). I am not sure, and in most cases, I can never be sure. To be sure would imply a judgment. I can only say for sure that this has been and is my emotional reaction.

If I were to tell you that I am annoyed by something you do, again I cannot be so arrogant as to think that your action would annoy anyone. I do not even mean that your action is in any way wrong or offensive. I simply mean that here and now I experience annoyance. Perhaps it is my headache or my indigestion or the fact that I did not get much sleep last night. I really do not know. All that I know is this, that I am trying to tell you that I am experiencing annoyance at this moment.

It would probably be helpful in most cases to preface our gut-level communication with some kind of a disclaimer to assure the other that there is no judgment implied. I might begin by saying, "I don't know why this bothers me, but it does . . . I guess I'm just hypersensitive. I really don't mean to imply that it is your fault, but I do feel hurt by what you are saying."

Of course, the main thing is that there is *in fact* no judgment. If I am in the habit of judging the intentions or motivation of another, I should try very hard to outgrow this immature habit. I

simply will not be able to disguise my judgments, no matter how many disclaimers I make.

   On the other hand, if I am really mature enough
to refrain from such judgments, this too will
eventually be apparent. If I really want to know
the intention or motivation or reaction of
another, there is only one way to find out: *I must
ask the person.* (Don't pass this by lightly. You
don't have X-ray eyes either!)

   Perhaps a word should be inserted here about
the difference between judging a person and
judging an action. If I see someone stealing
another's money, I can judge that this *action* is
morally wrong, but I cannot judge *the person.* It is
for God, not for you or me, to judge human
responsibility. If, however, we could not judge
the rightness or wrongness of an action in itself,
it would be the end of all objective morality. Let
us not fall into this, that there is nothing objec-
tively wrong or right, that it is all in the way you
look at it. However, to judge the responsibility of
another is playing God.

   Rule two: Emotions are not moral (good or bad).
Theoretically, most of us would accept the fact
that emotions are neither meritorious nor sinful.
Feeling frustrated, or being annoyed, or experiencing fears and anger does not make one a good
or a bad person. Practically, however, most of us
do not accept in our day-to-day living what

we would accept in theory. We exercise a rather strict censorship of our emotions. If our censoring conscience does not approve certain emotions, we repress these emotions into our subconscious mind. Experts in psychosomatic medicine say that the most common cause of fatigue and actual sickness is the repression of emotions. The fact is that there are emotions to which we do not want to admit. We are ashamed of our fears, or we feel guilty because of our anger or our emotional and physical desires.

Before we can be liberated enough to practice "gut-level communication," in which we will be emotionally open and honest, we must feel convinced that emotions are *not moral* but simply *factual.* My jealousies, my anger, my sexual desires, my fears, and so on, do not make me a good or bad person. Of course, these emotional reactions must be integrated by my mind and will. But before they can be integrated, before I can decide whether I want to act on them or not, I must allow them to arise and I must clearly hear what they are saying to me. I must be able to say, without any sense of moral reprehension, that I am afraid or angry or sexually aroused.

Before I will be free enough to do this, however, I must be convinced that emotions are not moral, neither good nor bad in themselves. I must be convinced, too, that the experience of the whole gamut of emotions is a part of the human condition, the inheritance of every human being.

Rule three: Feelings (emotions) must be integrated with the intellect and will. It is extremely important to understand this next point. The nonrepression of our emotions means that we must experience, recognize, and accept our emotions fully. It does not in any way imply that we will always *act on* those emotions. Allowing our feelings or emotions to control our lives would be tragic and the worst form of immaturity. It is one thing to feel and to admit to myself and to others that I am afraid, but it is another thing to allow this fear to overwhelm me. It is one thing for me to feel and to admit that I am angry, and another to punch you in the nose.

Will

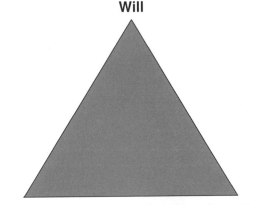

Intellect   **Feelings (emotions)**

In the triangle above we see the three human faculties that must be integrated, that is, brought into one harmonious wholeness, if one is to advance in the process of becoming a person. If the meaning of this integration is clear, it is

The behavior
of the fully human being
is always unpredictable --
simply because it is free.

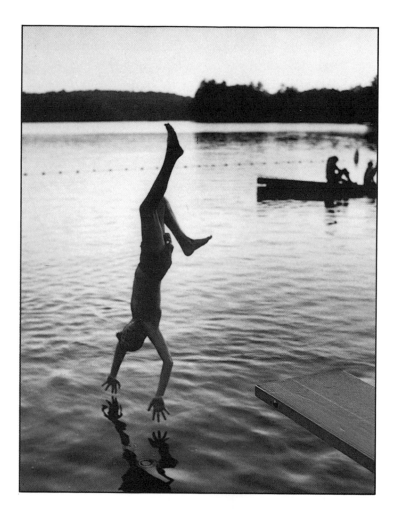

apparent that the mind judges the necessity or desirability of acting upon certain emotions that have been fully experienced. Then the will carries this judgment into effect. For example, I may feel a strong fear of telling you the truth in some given matter. The fact is, and it is neither good nor bad in itself, that I am experiencing fear. I allow myself to feel this fear fully, to recognize it as such. My mind makes the judgment that I should act not out of this fear but in spite of it, and that I should tell you the truth. The will consequently carries out the judgment of the mind. I tell you the truth.

However, if I am seeking a real and authentic relationship with you, and wish to practice "gut-level" communication, I must tell you something like this: "I really don't know why . . . maybe it's my streak of cowardice . . . but I feel afraid to tell you something, and yet I know that I must be honest with you . . . This is the truth as I see it . . ."

Or, to take another example, maybe I feel very tender and loving toward you. As Chesterton once remarked, the meanest fear of all is the fear of sentiment. Perhaps it is our cultural heritage or maybe it is the fear of rejection, but we often experience a great reluctance to be externally tender and loving. Perhaps in this case my mind will pass the judgment that it is right to act on this impulse of feeling, and again my will carries the judgment into execution. It should be obvious that in the integrated person, emotions are neither repressed nor do they assume control of the whole person. They are recognized (What is it that I am feeling?) and integrated (Do I want to act on this feeling or not?).

Rule four: In "gut-level" communication, emotions must be "reported." If I am to tell you who I really am, I must tell you about my feelings, whether I decide to act upon them or not. I may tell you that I am angry, explaining the fact of my anger without inferring any judgment of you, and not intending to act upon this anger. I may tell you that I am afraid, explaining the fact of my fear without accusing you of being its cause, and at the same time not succumbing to the fear. But I must, if I am to open myself to you, allow you to experience (encounter) my person and tell you about my anger and my fear.

It has been truly said that we either *speak out* (report) our feelings or we will *act them out.* Feelings are like steam that is gathering inside of a kettle. Kept inside and gathering strength, they can blow the human lid off, just as the steam inside of the kettle will blow off the lid of the kettle.

We have already referred to the verdict, handed down by psychosomatic medicine, that repressed emotions are the most common cause of fatigue and actual sickness. This is part of the "acting out" process. Repressed emotions may find their outlet in the "acting out" of headaches, skin rashes, allergies, asthma, common colds, aching backs or limbs. They can also be acted out in the tightening of muscles, the slamming of doors, the clenching of fists, the rising of blood pressure, the grinding of teeth, or in tears, temper tantrums, acts of violence. We do not bury our emotions *dead;* they remain *alive* in our subconscious minds and intestines, to hurt and trouble us. It is not only much more conducive to an authentic relationship to report our true feelings, but equally essential to our integrity and health.

The most common reason for not reporting our emotions is that we do not want to admit to them for one reason or another. We fear that others might not think well of us, or actually reject us, or punish us in some way for our emotional candor. We have been somehow "programmed" not to accept certain emotions as part of us. We are ashamed of them. Now we can rationalize and say that we cannot report these emotions because they would not be understood. We might reason that reporting them would disturb a peaceful relationship or evoke an emotionally stormy reaction from the other. But all of our reasons are essentially fraudulent, and our silence can produce only fraudulent relationships. Anyone who builds a relationship on less than openness and honesty is building on sand. Such a relationship will never stand the test of time, and neither party to the relationship will draw from it any noticeable benefits.

Rule five: With rare exceptions, emotions must be reported at the time that they are being experienced. It is much easier for most of us to report an emotion that is past, a matter of history. It is almost like talking about another person when I can talk about myself a year or two years ago, and admit that I was very fearful or very angry at that time. Because they were transient emotions and are now gone, it is easy to dissociate these feelings from my person here and now. It is difficult, however, to recapture a feeling once it has passed into my personal history. We are very often puzzled by such previous emotions. "I don't know why I ever got so excited." The time to report emotions is the time when they are being experienced. Even temporary deferral of this report of emotions is unwise and unhealthy.

All communication must obviously respect not only the transmitter of the communication but also the receiver who is to accept the communication. Consequently, it could occur that in the integration of my emotions, my judgment may dictate that this is not the opportune moment to report my emotional reaction. If the receiver is so emotionally disturbed that he or she could hardly be in a receptive mood, and my report

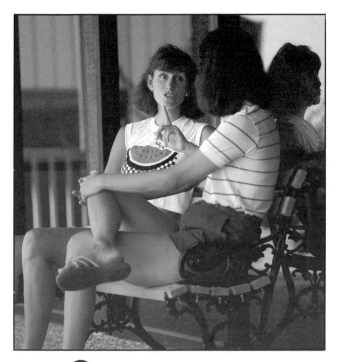

Whatever my secrets are,
remember
when I entrust them to you,
they are part of me.

would only be distorted somehow by the receiver's turbulent emotional state, it may be that I will have to defer this report.

But if the matter is serious enough and the emotions strong enough, this period of deferment cannot be too long nor can I be frightened or bullied into complete repression of emotions. Please note that this period of deferment should never be a long one. It would seem that in most cases shelving emotions even temporarily should be a rare thing.

However, it would seem to be a valid exception to this rule to defer or eliminate this report in the case of a passing incident with a chance acquaintance. The gruff manner of a bus driver may irk me, without this being the occasion for me to tell the driver about my emotional reactions to him or her. In the case of two people, however, who must work or live together or who want to relate deeply, this emotional reporting at the time of the emotions is seriously and vitally important.

THE BENEFITS OF "GUT-LEVEL" COMMUNICATION

The obvious and primary benefit of "gut-level" communication will be real and authentic relationship and what we have called a true "encounter" of persons. Not only will there be mutual communication of persons and the consequent sharing and experiencing of person-hood, but "gut-level" communication will result in a more and more clearly defined sense of self-identity for each of the parties in the relationship.

Today, many of us are asking: "Who am I?" It has come to be a socially fashionable question. The implication is that I do not really know my own self as a person. We have said that my person is what I think, judge, feel, and so on. If I have communicated these things freely and openly, as clearly as I can and as honestly as I can, I will find a noticeable growth in my own sense of identity. I will also experience a deeper and more authentic knowledge of my person. It has come to be an accepted psychological truism that I will understand only as much of myself as I have been willing to communicate to another.

The second and very important result of such communication is that, having understood myself because I have communicated myself, I will find the patterns of immaturity gradually changing into patterns of maturity. I will change! Anyone who sees the *patterns* of his or her reactions, and is willing to examine them, may come to the realization that these are patterns of hypersensitivity or paranoia. At the moment the realization penetrates, he or she will find the pattern changing. Notwithstanding all that we have said about emotions, we must not believe that emotional patterns are purely biological or inevitable. *I can and will change my emotional patterns;* that is, I will move from one emotion to another if I have honestly let my emotions arise for recognition and, having honestly reported them, judge them to be immature and inappropriate.

For example, if I consistently and honestly report the emotion of "feeling hurt" by many small and inconsequential things, it will become apparent to me in time that I am hypersensitive and that I have been indulging myself in self-pity. The moment that this becomes clear to me, really hits me, I will change.

In summary the dynamic is this: We allow our emotions to arise so that they can be identified; we observe the patterns in our emotional reactions and then we report and judge them. Having done these things, we instinctively and immediately make the necessary adjustments in the light of our own ideals and hopes for growth. We change. Try this and see for yourself. It works.

As has been said, our emotional reactions are not biological or psychological necessities. We can move from one emotion to another if we want to. Many examples could be added here. I can feel viciously competitive, but if I allow the emotions under my spirit of competition to surface for recognition, I may discover that it is only my sense of inferiority, my lack of belief in myself, that propels me into competition. It is strangely mysterious how, when these emotions are allowed to illuminate our inner selves, they can tell us things we never knew about ourselves. And this kind of self-knowledge is the beginning of growth.

Or I might be laboring with a destructive emotion like despair. If I allow it to arise for inspection, my despair will show itself to be merely an attempt at self-punishment. Much "depression" is simply self-punishment. Further self-investigation may show me that I have a guilt complex, and that I need this punishment to atone for my guilt feelings. I am on a course of self-destruction. When I can recognize these emotions as negative and self-destroying, it is then within my power to move to a new emotional reaction—from self-pity or self-punishment to love, from anger to empathy, from despair to hope.

If all this is true, and you have only to experience it to know its truth, it is obvious that the little phrase we have used so conveniently, "I'm sorry, but that's the way I am," is nothing more than a refuge and delusion. It is handy if you don't want to grow up; but if you do want to grow up, you try to rise above this fallacy.

The third benefit of "gut-level" communication is that it will evoke from others a responsive honesty and openness, which is necessary if the relationship is to be interpersonal, mutual. A psychiatrist friend of mine somewhat boastfully claims that he can gain instant access to the deepest parts of anyone within a matter of minutes. His technique is not to begin by probing with questions. This would only make the insecure person more defensive. The theory of this psychiatrist is that if we want another to be open with us, we must begin by opening up ourselves, by telling the other very honestly and openly of our feelings.

Person is resonant to person, psychologist Josef Goldbrunner insists. If I am willing to step out of the darkness of my prison, to expose the deepest part of me to other persons, the result is almost always automatic and immediate: The other persons feel empowered to reveal themselves to me. Having heard of my secret and deep feelings, others are given the courage to communicate themselves. This, in the last analysis, is what we meant by "encounter."

4

Dealing with Our Emotions

We have said that fully human people do not repress their emotions, as far as this is under their control, but allow them to rise to the surface of recognition. They experience the fullness of their emotional life; they are "in touch with," attuned to their emotions, aware of what their emotions are saying to them about their needs and their relationships with others. On the other hand, we have also said that this does not imply surrender to the emotions. In fully human people, there is a balance of senses, emotions, intellect, and will. The emotions have to be integrated. Though it is necessary to "report" our emotions, it is not at all necessary that we "act on" them. We must never allow our emotions to control our decisions.

The critical importance of all this will be clear to you if you will reflect for just a moment on the following: (1) Almost all the pleasures and pains

Most of us feel that others will not tolerate such emotional honesty in communication. We would rather defend our dishonesty on the grounds that it might hurt others. Having rationalized our phoniness into nobility, we settle for superficial relationships.

of life are deeply involved with the emotions. (2) Most human conduct is the result of emotional forces (even though we are all tempted to pose as pure intellects, and to explain on rational, objective grounds all of our preferences and actions). (3) Most interpersonal conflicts result from emotional stresses (for example, anger, jealousy, frustrations), and most interpersonal encounters are achieved through some kind of emotional communion (for example, empathy, tenderness, feelings of affection and attraction). In other words, your emotions and how you deal with them will probably make you or break you in the adventure of life.

The mechanics of "awareness," "reporting," and "integration" of the emotions may be illustrated as follows.

Situation: You are having a discussion with a member of your family or a friend. There are several differences of opinion, and very gradually voices and blood pressures rise. You are beginning to feel the stress of strong feelings. What should you do?

HEALTHY

1. Be aware of your emotions. Turn your mind briefly away from the argument and pay direct attention to your emotional reaction. Ask yourself: What am I feeling? Is it embarrassment (because the other person's arguments sound better)? Is it fear (the other person is pretty big and is getting more angry by the minute)? Superiority (because you're ahead on points, and he or she knows it)?

2. Admit your emotion. Turn your full awareness toward the emotion. Take a good look so that you can identify it. Estimate, too, how strong it is. It is anger, for example, and it is pretty high voltage, too.

3. Investigate your emotion. If you really want to find out a lot about yourself, ask your anger how it got there, and where it came from. Trace the origin of your emotion. You may not be able to uncover the whole family tree of your present emotion, but you just may get a glimpse of an inferiority complex to which you have never admitted.

UNHEALTHY

1. Ignore your emotional reaction. It has nothing to do with the argument anyway. Better yet (if you want to make the worst mistake), tell yourself that you're not getting upset at all. If you are perspiring, tell yourself that it's just warm in the room. Keep your anger down in the pit of your stomach, where your head can't notice it. Feeling emotions during an intellectual discussion is unworthy of you anyway.

2. Keep denying your emotions. Tell yourself and tell others, "But I'm not mad at all." Emotions are more easily ignored if you keep your mind fixed on the argument. Don't let your emotions distract you. You can take Alka Seltzer later, when your stomach calls you a liar.

3. Keep combing through your mind for rebuttal materials. The person with the right moves and bright lines is going to break this thing wide open. It's strictly win-lose now. Slow the words down; you're starting to sputter. But keep up a steady flow, or the other person will get in there and make a point. Keep your mind on the argument, and keep moving toward the jugular vein.

HEALTHY

4. Report your emotion. Just the facts now. No interpretations or judgments. "Let's cool it for a minute. I'm getting too worked up, and I'm starting to say things I really don't mean." It is very important not to accuse or judge in this report. Do not tell the other person that it is his or her fault that you got so angry. It really isn't, you know. It's something in you. Don't blame the other person even to yourself.

5. Integrate your emotion. Having listened to your emotion, and having questioned it and reported it, now let your mind judge what is the right thing to do, and let your will carry out the judgment. For example, "Let's start again. I think I've been too defensive to listen to you. I'd like to try again." Or, "Would you mind if we dropped the subject? I'm afraid I'm getting too touchy to discuss anything."

UNHEALTHY

4. If you should blow your cool completely and become incoherent, blame it on the other person. And be sure to include some deep personality defect in your indictment. For example, "It's impossible to discuss anything with you. You're too damned arrogant. You never (generalizations like this are good, too) listen. You think you're God, don't you?" (Make sure he or she knows that the question is rhetorical.)

5. Since you haven't even admitted to having an emotion, you won't have to go through the trouble of trying to learn from your emotional reactions or integrating them. Repressed emotions, however, have a way of acting up, so walk out in a huff, and take a couple of aspirins—and keep your mind on how unreasonable the other person was.

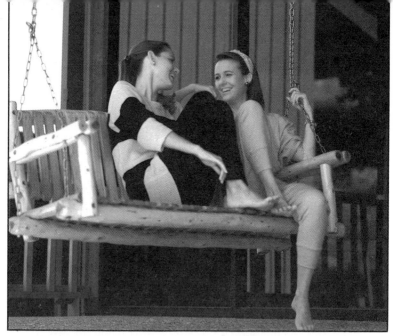

To tell you my *THOUGHTS*
is to locate myself
in a category.

To tell you about my
feelings is to tell
you about me.

REFLECTIONS ON "ESTRANGEMENT" AND "ENCOUNTER"

In spite of our unwillingness and reluctance to tell others who we are, there is in each one of us a deep and driving desire to be understood. It is clear to all of us that we want very badly to be loved, but when we are not understood by those whose love we need and want, any sort of deep communication becomes a nervous and uncomfortable thing. It does not enlarge and enliven us. It becomes clear that others cannot really love us effectively unless they really understand us. People who feel that they are understood, however, will almost certainly feel that they are loved.

If there is no one who understands me, and who accepts me for what I am, I will feel "estranged." My talents and possessions will not comfort me at all. Even in the midst of many people, I will always carry within me a feeling of isolation and aloneness. I will experience a kind of "solitary confinement." It is a law, as certain as the law of gravity, that those who are understood and loved will grow as persons; those who are estranged will die in their cell of solitary confinement, alone.

There are many things inside every one of us that we would like to share. All of us have our own secret past, our secret shames and broken dreams, our secret hopes. Over and against this need and desire to share these secrets and to be understood, every one of us must weigh fear and risk. Whatever my secrets are, they seem, more than anything else, to be deeply and uniquely a part of me. No one has ever done the precise things that I have done; no one has ever thought my thoughts or dreamed my dreams. I am not sure that I could even find the words to share these things with another, but what I am even less sure of is this: How would they sound to another?

People who have a good self-image, who really and truly accept themselves, will be greatly helped at this time of dilemma. It is not very likely, however, that those who have never really shared themselves could have the support of a good self-image. Most of us have experienced and done things, have lived with sensations and feelings, that we feel we would never dare tell another. To the other, I might appear deluded or even evil, ridiculous or vain. My whole life could appear as a hideous deceit.

A thousand fears keep us in the solitary con-finement of estrangement. In some of us there is the fear of breaking down, of sobbing like a child. Others of us feel restrained by the fear that the other person will not sense the tremendous importance that our secret has for us. I usually anticipate how deep the pain would be if my secret were met with apathy, misunderstanding, shock, anger, or ridicule. My confidant might become angry or reveal my secret to others for whom it was not intended.

It may have happened that, at some point in my life, I took some part of me out of the darkness and placed it in the light for the eyes of another. It may be that this other person did not understand, and I ran full of regrets into a painful emotional solitude. Yet, there may have been other moments when someone heard my secret and accepted my confidence in gentle hands. I may remember what that person said to assure me, the compassion in his or her voice, the understanding look in his or her eyes. I remember what those eyes looked like. I remember how the individual's hand took mine. I remember the gentle pressure that told me I was understood. It was a great and liberating experience, and in its wake I felt so much more alive. An immense need had been answered in me to be really listened to, to be taken seriously, and to be understood.

It is only through this kind of sharing that we come to *know ourselves*. Introspection of itself is helpless. We can confide all of our secrets to the docile pages of a personal diary, but we can know ourselves and experience the fullness of life only in the sharing with another person. Friendship becomes a great adventure. There is a continuously deeper discovery of myself and my friend as we continue to reveal new and deeper layers of ourselves. It opens my mind, widens my horizons, fills me with new awareness, deepens my feelings, gives my life meaning.

Yet the barriers are never permanently broken. Friendship and mutual self-revelation have a newness about them with each new day, because being a human person involves daily change and growth. You and I are growing, and our differences are becoming more apparent. We are not growing into the same person, but I am growing into my own person and you into yours. I discover in you other tastes and preferences, other feelings and hopes, other reactions to new experiences. I discover that this business of telling you who I am cannot be done once and for all. I must *continually* tell you who I am and you must *continually* tell me who you are, because both of us are continually evolving.

It may be that the very things that first attracted me to you now seem to work against communication. In the beginning, your sentiment seemed to balance off my more intellectual inclinations; your extroverted ways complemented my introversion; your realism counterbalanced my artistic intuition. It seemed like such an ideal friendship. We seemed like separate halves that needed each other to become one whole. But now, when I want you to share my intellectual

Fully human people are in deep and
meaningful contact with
the world outside of them.

They listen not only to themselves
but to the voices of their world.
The breadth of their own individual
experience is infinitely multiplied
through a sensitive empathy with others.
They suffer with the suffering,
rejoice with the joyful.
They are born again every springtime,
feel the impact of the great mysteries of
life: birth, growth, love, suffering, death.
Their hearts skip along with the "young
lovers,"and they know something
of the exhilaration that is in them.
They also know the ghetto's philosophy
of despair, the loneliness of suffering
without relief. The bell never tolls
without tolling in some strange way
for them.

vision, I am annoyed that you take no interest in
my objective arguments of reason. Now, when I
want to show you that you are not logical in your
sentiment, it does not seem to matter at all to you.
In the beginning we seemed to fit together so
well. Now your desire to go out to others and my
more introverted inclinations to seek solitude
seem to be divisive.

Of course, our friendship can still be. We are
standing within arms' reach of that which is most
humanly rewarding and beautiful. We must not
turn back now. We can still share all the things
we once shared with such excitement, when first I
told you who I was and you told me who you
were. Only now our sharing will be deeper
because we are deeper. If I will continue to hear
you with the same sense of wonder and joy as I
did in the beginning, and you will hear me in this
way, our friendship will grow firmer and deeper
roots. The tinsel of our first sharing will mellow
into gold. We can and will be sure that there is no
need to hide anything from each other. We will
have shared everything.

I am continually experiencing the ever-growing,
ever-new reality of you, and you are experiencing
the reality of me. And through each other, we are
together experiencing the reality of God, who
once said that "it is not good for man to be alone."

your slightest look
easily will unclose me
though i have closed myself as fingers,
you open always petal by petal
myself as spring opens
(touching skillfully, mysteriously)
her first rose

e. e. cummings

5

Human Hiding Places: Methods of Ego-defense

Before proceeding to a catalog of various roles and games, it seems necessary to say something about the methods of ego-defense, which are always somehow involved in these roles and games. In brief, these ego-defenses are compensations cultivated to counterbalance and camouflage something else in us which we consider a defect or a handicap.

The great Alfred Adler first became interested in *compensation* as a psychological phenomenon when he noticed how human nature tends to make up for bodily deficiencies. One kidney takes over the function of two if one fails to function. The same thing is true of lungs. A bone fracture that heals properly makes the place of the fracture become stronger than normal.

It is also true that many famous people have developed some skill to an extraordinary degree precisely because they were trying to overcome some handicap. Glenn Cunningham, the first of the famous American mile runners, probably became such a great runner trying to strengthen his legs which were seriously crippled at age seven in a fire that almost took his life. Wilma Rudolph contracted polio as a small child and finally learned to walk without braces. She later began to run, and at the 1960 Olympics in Rome she became the first woman to receive three gold metals in track and field. There is also what is called "vicarious compensation," by which a person handicapped in one way learns to excel in another. Whistler, the famous painter, flunked out of West Point and forfeited his desires for a career in the military, but learned to excel as an artist by developing his talents in that field.

REACTION FORMATION

The "reaction formation," which we are considering here, is an overcompensation by exaggerating or overdeveloping certain conscious trends. It is developed as a defense against unconscious tendencies of an opposite and unapprovable character, which threaten to break into conscious recognition. Extremely dogmatic people, who are absolutely sure of everything, consciously cultivate this posture of certainty because of demoralizing doubts in their subconscious mind. Their self-image isn't strong enough to live with these doubts. People who are overly tender, to the point of exaggerated sentimentality, are usually suspected of assuming this attitude in compensation for harsh and cruel tendencies that have been repressed into the subconscious mind.

Prudishness, in an exaggerated form, is usually an overcompensation for repressed normal sexual desires with which the prude cannot live in comfort. The person who seems to exert an exaggerated concern for the health of an aged parent probably does so to compensate for the subconscious desire to be freed of responsibility for that parent by the death of the same.

Please note well that we cannot suspect every good inclination of being a psychological cover-up for opposite inclinations. The thing about reaction formation is that it is always an over-compensation, an exaggerated reaction. Compensatory attitudes are a leaning over backward to avoid tipping forward. This kind of compensation, once set in motion, always results in an exaggeration or excess. It is, consequently, only exaggerated behavior of any kind that is suspect of being compensatory "reaction formation." The dogmatist is never wrong. The prude is hyperchaste. The reformer-type, preachy and self-righteous, viciously hates sin and sinner alike without any recognition of normal human weakness.

It is socially fashionable
to ask: Who am I?
There is no little
"real self"
inside of me.
I am what I am committed to.

The conclusion is this: *Exaggerated behavior* in a person usually means *just the opposite* of what it implies. Very often we accuse dogmatists of pride and feel "called" to help them learn sweet humility. In fact, they are not at all sure of themselves, and the more we try to defeat them, to cultivate doubts in them and expose their errors, the more they have to compensate. Their dogmatism will probably become even more extreme and obnoxious.

DISPLACEMENT

A second ego-defense mechanism is called "displacement." It usually refers to the indirect expression of an impulse that the censoring conscience (Freud's *superego*) prohibits us from expressing directly. For example, a child may develop a seething hostility toward his or her parents. Our social programming usually will not allow direct expression of this hostility. I mean, you can't hate your own parents. So, not in touch with the hostility that the child felt forced to repress, he or she smashes public property, bullies younger children, or does something equally irrational. The apparent homicidal-minded boxing fan, who stands up at ringside and vociferously yells "Murder the bum!" as a helpless, senseless boxer is sinking to his knees, obviously harbors some subconscious hostility. The anger had to be repressed because the person just couldn't live with it or express it.

"Scapegoating" is a common form of displacement. We react with uncalled-for violence when
someone looks at us the wrong way, because
there is a hostility in us that we cannot express
directly. For some reason the person to whom we
would like to express hostility seems too
formidable to us. A man with a violent temper in
the office may well be expressing the hostility he
feels for his wife or for himself but cannot bring
himself to express it at home. Or the woman who
has been unjustly upbraided by her employer (of
whom she is afraid because her job is at stake)
may come home and take out her hostility on her
husband and children. Prudes, who cannot admit
to their sexual drives directly, will take great
interest in "scandals" of a sexual nature. Lonely,
isolated individuals, who cannot admit directly
to their need for love and affection, will profess
to be "madly in love" with someone else (whom
they do not really love at all).

A second meaning of "displacement" is the
device of disguising unpleasant realities to which
we cannot admit (and therefore repress) by
consciously stressing something else which is not
so embarrassing to the ego. We profess to worry
about some triviality to conceal some greater fear
to which we cannot honestly admit. Or let us say
that I am jealous of you, but I cannot really admit
it, not even to myself. So I "zero in" on some
trivial annoyance, like the quality of your voice. I
find it very grating. The husband and wife who

have come to despise each other, but cannot
openly admit to the real sources of their mutual
agony, usually bicker about trivialities with great
vehemence.

The man whose mother dominated his father is
usually programmed to treat his own wife as an
inferior. However, he cannot admit to his resentment for his mother and her treatment of his
father, or that he definitely wants his wife
"under" him. So he will usually complain about
small and inconsequential habits of hers. He will
deny the value of her opinions and the wisdom
of her actions. He will bitterly criticize her for the
"stupid way" she plays cards.

PROJECTION

Another ego-defense mechanism is called
"projection." All of us tend to disown things in
ourselves and to "project" them into others. We
try to rid ourselves of our own limitations by
attributing them to someone else. Adam ex-
plained his sin to God by saying, "The woman
tempted me." Eve ascribed the whole calamity to
the serpent. It is also projection when we blame
other things for our own failures, like the
circumstances, the tools we had to work with, the
position of the stars. We are tempted to ask,
"Why don't you look where you're going?"
when we bump into people.

It is a very common human inclination (projection) to dislike most in others what we cannot accept in ourselves. The real mystery of this projection is that we don't recognize these things in ourselves. They have been repressed. We can therefore strongly condemn in others what we cannot admit in ourselves. The stronger and the more exaggerated the dislike of anything or any quality is manifested, the more it might be suspected as projection.

When we get a bug on "hypocrisy," and often condemn it, and proclaim that it is widespread among the human race, it is most probable that we must repress all conscious recognition that we ourselves are hypocritical. Vain people, who can't admit to their own inclinations, suspect everybody of wanting attention and publicity. Ambitious men and women, who cannot honestly admit (and therefore repress) their own driving ambitions, usually feel that "everybody is out for No. 1; all that most people want is fame and money."

Then there are the paranoids (persecution complex victims) who project their own self-hatred into other people and feel that others don't like them. Prudes think that every attractive person of the opposite sex is making improper advances; they project their own concealed (repressed) longings into others. People with an uneasy conscience feel that others are suspicious of them, watching them. Very often, too, when someone puts a finger on a weakness in us, for example, being too temperamental, we counter by charging, "You're the one who is too temperamental!"

INTROJECTION

"Introjection" is the ego-defense by which we attribute to ourselves the good qualities of others. Introjection is prominent in what we call "hero worship." We identify with our heroes. Also, we identify our possessions with ourselves. We take great pride when someone praises our home, or we think that we are "big time" because we come from a famous city, belong to a well-known fraternity, or have traveled to many places. Many women identify with the tragic heroines of soap-opera programs on television. A Manhattan psychiatrist noticed that very many of his women patients had relapses after becoming addicted to these shows. They identified with all the unhappiness of the suffering characters in these melodramas. This kind of identification provides an easy access into a world of fantasy and provides romance in our lives. However, often the result of this ego-defense is neither very profitable nor very consoling.

RATIONALIZATION

The most common form of ego-defense is "rationalization." As a technique for self-justification, it is hard to beat. We find some reason for our action that justifies it. We "think" (rationalize) our way to a preordained conclusion. Very often there are two reasons for everything we do: the alleged good reason and the real reason. Rationalization not only results in self-deceit but eventually corrupts all sense of integrity (wholeness). We rationalize our failures; we find justification for our actions; we reconcile our ideals and deeds; we make our emotional preferences our rational conclusions. I say that I drink beer because it has malt in it. The real reason is that I like it; it helps me feel uninhibited and secure with others.

As with all ego-defense mechanisms, there is always something that I cannot admit in myself, something that I would like to do which appears wrong, or something that would make me feel better if only I could just believe it. Rationalization is the bridge that makes my wishes the facts. It is the use of intelligence to deny the truth; it makes us dishonest with ourselves. And if we cannot be honest with ourselves, we certainly cannot be honest with anyone else. Rationalization consequently sabotages all human authenticity. It disintegrates and fragments the personality.

Insincerity, as an interior state of mind, is a psychological impossibility. I can't tell myself that I do and don't believe something at the same

To understand people,
I must try to hear
what they are <u>not</u> saying,
what they perhaps
will never be able to say.

time. Choosing evil as evil is also a psychological impossibility, because the will can only choose the (apparent) good. Consequently, to deny the truth I cannot admit, and to do the deed I cannot approve, I must necessarily rationalize until the truth is no longer true and the evil becomes good.

Did you ever ask yourself the surprisingly difficult question: How does one choose evil? How do we commit sin? The will can choose, by its very nature, only that which is somehow good. I am personally convinced that the exercise or use of free will in a given situation of guilt is this: The will, desirous of some evil that has good aspects (if I steal your money, I will be rich), forces the intellect to concentrate on the good to be acquired in the evil act. The will impels the mind to turn away from the recognition of evil. And so the intellect must rationalize that which was originally recognized as evil. While I am doing something wrong (in the act of doing it), I cannot be squarely facing its evil aspect; I must somehow be thinking of it as good and right. Consequently, free will seems to be exercised in the act of coercing the intellect to rationalize rather than in the execution of the act itself.

CAUTION: HUMAN BEINGS

In all of these ego-defense mechanisms, please notice that there is something that people who operate the mechanism have felt the necessity of repressing. They cannot live with some realization. In one way or another, they keep their psychological pieces intact by some form of self-deception. They just couldn't live comfortably with the truth, so they repressed it.

Therefore, and this is extremely important, the vocation of putting people straight, of tearing off their masks, of forcing them to face the repressed truth, is a highly dangerous and destructive calling. Eric Berne warns against disillusioning people about their "games." It may be that they just can't take it. They sought out some role, began playing some game, took to wearing some mask, precisely because this would make life livable and tolerable.

So we must be very careful, extremely careful in fact, that we do not assume the vocation of acquainting others with their delusions. We are all tempted to unmask others, to smash their defenses, to leave them naked and blinking in the light of the illumination provided by our exposé. It could be tragic in its results. If the psychological pieces come unglued, who will pick them up and put poor Humpty Dumpty Human Being together again? Will you? Can you?

THE GREATEST KINDNESS: THE TRUTH

All that has been said in these pages would urge us to be open and truthful about ourselves, our thoughts and emotions. It has urged us to be honest with ourselves and with others. Nothing is taken back here. But it is absolutely necessary to realize that nothing in these pages asks me or justifies me in becoming a judge of others. I can tell you who I am, report my emotions to you with candor and honesty, and this is the greatest kindness I can extend to myself and to you. Even if my thoughts and emotions are not pleasing to you, it remains the greatest kindness to reveal myself openly and honestly. Insofar as I am able, I will try to be honest with myself and communicate myself honestly to you.

It is another thing to set myself up as judge of your delusions. This is playing God. I must not try to be the guarantor of your integrity and honesty: that is your work. I can only hope that my honesty with and about myself will empower you to be honest with and about yourself. If I can face and tell you my faults and vanities, my hostilities and fears, my secrets and my shames, perhaps you will be able to admit to your own and confide them to me, if and when you wish.

It is a two-way street. If you will be honest with me, report your triumphs and tragedies, agonies and ecstasies to me, it will help me to face my

own. You will help me to become a real person. I
need your openness and honesty; you need mine.
Will you help me? I promise that I will try to help
you. I will try to tell you who I really am.

"It costs so much to be a full human being that there
are very few who have the enlightenment, or the
courage, to pay the price. . . . One has to abandon
altogether the search for security, and reach out to the
risk of living with both arms. One has to embrace the
world like a lover. One has to accept pain as a
condition of existence. One has to count doubt and
darkness as the cost of knowing. One needs a will
stubborn in conflict, but apt always to total
acceptance of every consequence of living and dying."

Morris L. West
in *The Shoes of the Fisherman*

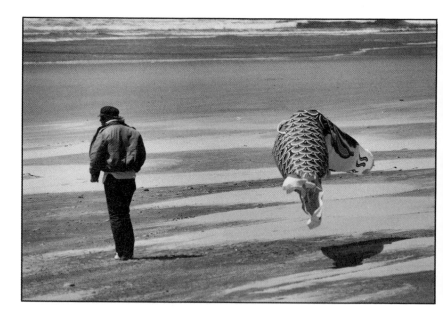

NO ONE ELSE CAN
DECIDE HOW
YOU ARE GOING
TO ACT.

YOU MUST MARCH
TO YOUR
OWN DRUMS.

6

Catalog of Games and Roles

There is no logical order in this partial listing of the roles and games that are very common patterns in human relations. Nor are there any restrictions as to sex or age. Anyone can play one or more of these games. The ones you and I become proficient at or employ most often will depend upon our "programming" and needs.

These games have one thing in common, no matter how different they may seem; they mask and distort the truth about the one most important thing that I could share with you: myself. I must ask myself: Which of these games do I play? What am I seeking? What am I hiding? What am I trying to win?

ALL HEART

What Freud called "reaction formation" is thought to be responsible for the excessively tender and sentimental concern of these people. It is a subconscious compensation for their sadistic (cruel) tendencies. We all have cruel inclinations at times, but these people are particularly horrified by theirs.

The one thing about compensation is that once it is set in motion, it nearly always results in overcompensation. Somehow their programming has rendered these people unable to be in touch with themselves. "All Hearters" just can't admit to their hostile inclinations, and they spend most of their energy denying the truth they cannot admit. These people are likely to be excessively tender to pets, overindulgent with children, excessively demonstrative in showing affection and tenderness.

"All heart" people follow the heart in all matters, to the point that others wonder if the head is operative at all. The heart decides everything. They can show all kinds of soft emotions, but will rarely if ever report harsher emotions precisely because they are afraid of such emotions and must keep them repressed. Women are more inclined to this "reaction formation" because our society programs them to believe that hostile or cruel emotions are particularly horrifying in a woman.

ALWAYS RIGHT

These people rarely if ever lose an argument.
Even when the evidence begins to stack up
against them, they can salvage respect for their
position. They do not listen well and give the
appearance of expecting to learn little if anything
from others. Basically, their self-esteem is
threatened. Their dogmatism, like excessive
tenderness, is a result of reaction formation. They
act doubly certain in order to guard against
demoralizing doubts that stir in their
subconscious and tend to undermine their
certainty. Their behavior indicates the opposite
of what seems to be true. They have deep, if
subconscious, doubts about themselves and
their opinions.

BODY BEAUTIFUL, THE

Usually physical vanity is a compensation for a gnawing sense of inferiority as a person. The beautiful or handsome people who play this game keep staring into the mirror on the wall and into the mirror of the eyes of others (or in any shiny surface), looking for their own reflection. They do this because they cannot find any deeper consolations. There is a sadness that hangs over vanity of this sort. Life is obviously over at thirty-five. In the extreme, these people identify their person with their body. They would answer the question "What are you?" with the response "I'm good-looking." And if they could be honest and open, they would add: ". . . nothing more, just good-looking."

BRAGGART, THE

This game is a childish attempt to assert one's superiority. It is one of the various manifestations of arrested emotional development. The braggart is usually a bully, too, if the situation allows. Braggarts want to dominate others, either by words or, if they feel sure of themselves, by physical strength. The indication is lack of self-esteem. They want to feel important and discover nothing in themselves that satisfies this need. We sometimes are tempted to ask them: "Are you trying to convince us or yourself?" The answer is: both.

The games we play always follow the program.

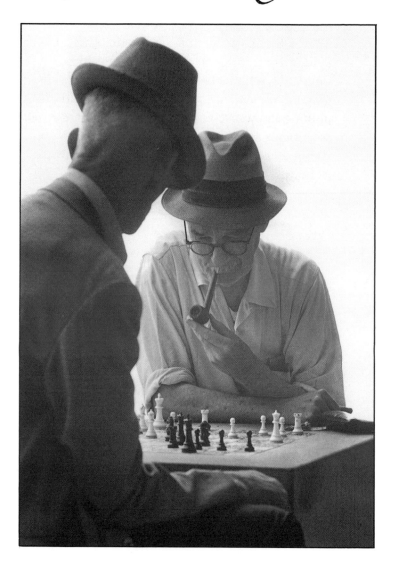

CLOWN, THE

Compulsive clowns are, like most of us, seeking some sort of recognition and attention. The sadness is that they think they can gain notice only by playing the fool for others. Deeper than this, it may be that they identify with their act and try to escape reality by taking nothing seriously. Clowning is sometimes an escape device. Clowns don't know how to handle themselves in a serious situation or how to react to sorrow, so they adopt an attitude of irresponsible gaiety. In dealing with others, their clowning serves as an adequate defensive mask (like the mask of the circus clown) to prevent others from knowing who they really are. They would rather laugh and joke than face the grim realities of life. They would rather put their act on the stage than lay their person on the line.

COMPETITOR, THE

Our American culture has programmed most of us to accept competition as a part of some divine plan. Competitors must win at whatever they do. They make everything a "win-lose" situation. They don't discuss; they debate. The triumphs that they seek, so often at the expense of others ("Nice guys finish last!"), may be the outgrowth of emotional deprivation or lack of approval earlier in life. The resultant insecurity causes them to question their worth, and they are consistently trying to prove this worth in competition and rivalry. Their need for recognition intensifies the drive to "get ahead." Competitors feel hostility toward anyone they feel is standing in their way or surpassing them. Sooner or later, they will be overcome by a sense of failure since the appetite for victory becomes increasingly voracious. They have, in the end, failed to prove their superiority and end up in frustration. Basically, the problem is that they cannot distinguish between themselves as persons and their accomplishments, between being and having. (See "Inferior and Guilty," below.)

CONFORMIST, THE

This game is called "peace at any price," and the price is surrender of all individuality to others. It usually begins with domineering authority and guilt feelings. Conformists won't or can't risk the nonacceptance of others. They are often praised for their willingness to "go along," but they pay a high price in repressed emotions for the pittances of praise that they receive. Their unwillingness to disagree with the established or fashionable opinion renders them an anonymity to others. They usually develop some sort of psycho-somatic symptoms because their subconscious mind eventually becomes overloaded with all that they have had to repress in order to be "the good guy/gal who goes along with anything." (See "Inferior and Guilty," below.)

CRANK, THE

The neurotic tendency that characterizes the crank is a low frustration tolerance. Cranks don't do very well in situations of strain and stress. Usually their programming, like that of competitors, involves early emotional deprivation, resulting in feelings of hostility. Cranks feel deprived of personal security. They feel less sure of themselves when things go wrong and nurse a long list of pet peeves, which they publish for others from time to time. Those in their vicinity know that any one of these can send them into orbit, and this is the game aspect. Others are warned in various ways that they must not frustrate cranks.

CYNIC, THE

The excessive expectations of life often collapse and result in the cynic game. People who are programmed to think that the universe should be tailored to their comfort often suffer a painful collision with reality. At this point, they strike back with their cynicism. Basically, cynics are demoralized unrealists. Things have failed to turn out the way they wanted them, and so cynics take their pains of disillusion out on everyone. You can't trust anyone. The whole system is corrupt. As long as they persist in their role as cynic, they won't have to take an honest look at themselves and their world nor go through the pains of adjustment to reality. Their facile wit is usually a symptom of submerged antagonism; they have not found life as they wanted it. They have never learned empathy or tolerance, and they have never experienced a true affection for others. Consequently, they are very lonely people behind their sardonic "smirks."

DELUDED BY GRANDEUR

This game usually grows out of a mistaken sense of personal importance. Players have been programmed to portray to others a sense of importance. They are name-droppers and tend to be "I-centered" in conversation. Like braggarts, these people play a game of compensation for inadequate self-esteem. There is always some effort to protect the wounded ego from further humiliation. They are attracted to dramatic deeds—a grandstander. They resent insignificance. They usually dream about some magnificent memento by which the world will remember them when they are gone. The delusional system tries to afford them a sense of importance denied in reality. Obviously, it is difficult to be honest with them about themselves.

DOMINATOR, THE

This game is often characterized by an exaggerated desire to control the lives of others as well as their thought processes. Like most people who exaggerate their importance or wisdom, dominators are bothered by sub-conscious feelings of inadequacy. It is strange that very often such people are so determined to feel adequate that they are distracted from the fact of their domineering ways. They usually explain their domination as necessary, reasonable, and justifiable. Dominators are very often troubled by feelings of hostility. These feelings, which they repress, find expression in selfishness and thoughtlessness in dealing with those they are supposed to love.

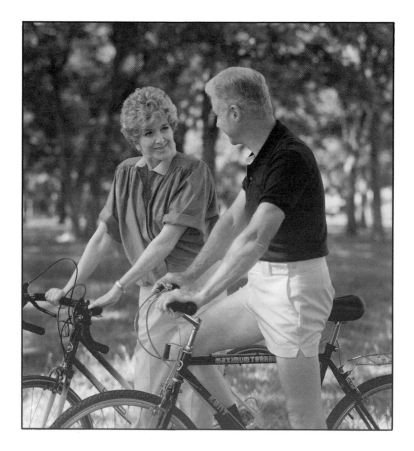

It is a law of human life,
as certain as gravity:
To live fully, we must
learn to _use_ things and _love_
people... not _love_ things
and _use_ people.

DREAMER, THE

This game is clearly an "escape" game. Dreamers are intent upon flight from reality. They achieve great things in a fantasy world, where they receive recognition and honor. Very often their dreams are a substitute for achievement and represent some kind of compensation for their lack of success with and in the real world. Dreamers usually like movies and stories because such flights of fancy stoke their imaginations with new settings and materials for future reveries. Eventually, they create a comfortable world in which they can become "somebody." Very often dreamers have ambitioned more than their abilities could reach, and they have to compensate themselves in fantasy for their disappointment in reality. This is sometimes called "neurotic fiction." Dreamers have an alibi to explain every actual failure. They can't bring their ambitions into line with their abilities. What they need most is the courage to accept themselves as they are.

DRINKER, THE PROBLEM, AND DOPE ADDICT, THE

The dreamer escapes from reality on the magic rug of fantasy; the drinker tries the route of narcosis. Those who are most vulnerable to stress are usually most in need of an escape. Addiction to drink or narcotic drugs is usually found in those who react poorly to deprivation, who are most easily overcome by defeat, and who are most self-conscious and ill at ease with others. This is not to deny, of course, that addiction is or can be genetic.

The momentary release and the experience of freedom, enjoyed under the sedation of excessive drink or dope, are usually followed by heightened anxiety and deeper depression when the haze clears. This, of course, brings on further need of sedation to deaden anxiety, the sense of guilt, and depression. Drinking and dope as a "way out" are definitely limited in their capacity to do the job. Leaving reality, while the narcosis lasts, only makes it more difficult to return to reality and to live with it. The name of the game is a "crutch" for sociability, self-expression, the concealment of embarrassment, and the possibility of forgetting one's troubles.

FLIRT, THE

The "flirting game" is basically an attempt to gain for the ego some kind of recognition. It is usually played by those who have never cultivated any real emotional depth. Only deeper relationships can result in security for the ego. Such relationships effect this security by promoting better self-knowledge and self-acceptance. Flirts, however, refuse to take the gamble of these more self-revealing relationships; they keep running.

Flirting is possible only when the emotions are trivial and superficial, though no one wants to admit this about his or her emotions. Stable and deeper human relationships can never be built on such emotions. The flirting game also assumes that when one tires of one conquest, he or she can move on to another. This is, of course, a rather selfish kind of sport, in which there are many injuries. No one wants to admit to being a flirt (or to playing any one of these games), but it is the first step to real emotional growth when we admit the tendency in order to hold it in some kind of check.

In all of these games, we must ask ourselves what it is that we really want, why we want it (which will always tell us something about ourselves), and why it would be better to give up our game. While flirting can bring some passing gratification to the ego, little fleeting infatuations often complicate life considerably. They lead us into subterfuges, the invention of excuses, deceits, and preoccupation with self. Sexual and emotional development starts with narcissism (self-fascination) in the child, but with growth as a person, one should become more and more capable of altruism (love of others). Flirts have been somehow fixated in an adolescent, self-centered state, and their growth has been arrested.

FRAGILE—HANDLE WITH CARE

Fragile people give many advance signals to others that they are delicate and need to be handled with great caution. Others are reluctant to confront people who have ready-to-go tear ducts and are capable of instant depressions. No one wants to deliver bad news to them, to ask them to accept responsibility (it is much easier to take it on yourself), or to offer them honest criticism. Fundamentally, this game grows out of a neurotic feeling of inability to cope with life. Fragility players exhibit a great sensitivity, too, to the estimate of others. Their ego is tender; remarks or gestures are often misinterpreted. Fragile people are hypersensitive precisely because they place very little value on themselves. This, however, will usually not be clear to themselves or to most others.

Fragility represents a regression to childhood, to a state of need and helplessness. If the game is played successfully, the players will never have to grow up or face the blood, sweat, and tears of real life. Fragile people express with their sudden tears and traumas what children say with their tantrums and screaming. The demand is for the preferential treatment children so often require.

GOSSIP, THE

Participants in the gossip game, like most game players, are in there for sensitive, personal stakes. Unable to make the full use of their own abilities, and being defeatists at heart and sorry for themselves because they cannot measure up to their own ego ideal, they choose to elevate their own self-esteem by undermining the esteem of others. Adler calls it the "derogatory critique." It is much easier to tear down others than to lift one's self up by achievement. Superiority and inferiority being relative terms, lowering others seems to raise one's own status.

Benjamin Franklin once said that if you want to know someone's faults, praise the person to his or her peers. Gossiping can also be a salve for sensitive guilt feelings. We like to recite the misdeeds of others so we won't have to feel so bad about our own misdeeds. This accounts for our eagerness to learn the latest scandals from newspapers, magazines, and so on. The media readily oblige and comfort the gossip. After reading about vicious murders, for example, our own sarcasm and anger do not seem to be such terrible evils. The gain of the game: elevation of self and greater ease in living with one's regrets.

HEDONIST, THE

"My pleasure before all" type people try to hide their emotional immaturity under various euphemisms ("just for 'kicks!'"), but the immaturity surfaces quickly in relationships. It is characteristic of the child and the neurotic (the emotional child) that they must have their pleasure and have it immediately. They will not inhibit for long any impulse to indulge themselves. They are not able to suspend their grasping for pleasure even long enough to look at the implications of their actions.

The inability to postpone pleasure eventually leads hedonists to seek their pleasure in all things, at anyone's expense. When the stimulus of pleasure-to-be-had is registered, the response is automatic. Habits of hedonism are very often acquired as compensatory for the difficult aspects of life. "I was overlooked or misunderstood, so now I can overeat or masturbate." (Such logic is almost never examined consciously.)

I...I...I

It is almost a universal law that the extent of egocentrism in any person is proportionate to the amount of pain in him or her. It is a question of attention. We cannot give a great deal of attention to ourselves and to others simultaneously. We have only a limited amount of attention that we can confer. The destructive or diminishing part of pain is that it magnetizes attention to ourselves and to the area of our pain. Those who are suffering anything from a toothache to the loneliness of old age tend to egocentrism. Preoccupation with self often evolves into hypochondria (overconcern with health) or paranoia (persecution complex).

People cannot fashion themselves to be the center of the universe and then live comfortably with the fact that others do not accept them as such. Whatever pains our past programming has left in us (guilt, inferiority, anxiety, and so on), these pains will inevitably lead us into all the pitfalls of egocentrism. Egocentrics do not mind what the conversation is about as long as it is about them. Eventually, they will fall into emotional depression because living in such a restricted world is living in a prison. They will suffer even more than the others who must live or work with them.

INDECISIVE AND UNCERTAIN

It has been said that the greatest mistake a person can make is to be afraid of making mistakes. Indecision and uncertainty are ways of avoiding mistakes and responsibility. If no decision is made, nothing can go wrong. The inclination to avoid decisions is sometimes manifested by dragging out as long as possible the ones we actually must make. The only real mistake is not to learn from our mistakes.

The basic problem here is self-esteem and the protection of self-esteem. People who are indecisive fear that they will lose respect if their decision turns out to be wrong. Only little people, someone has said, are never wrong. We learn more from our mistakes than from our successes. But indecisive people are so focused on their own egos and personal value that they do not see the validity of all these truths. The name of the game is safety and self-protection; the motto: Nothing attempted, nothing lost.

Very often, too, indecisiveness results in people who have been programmed by multitudinous (and sometimes contradictory) instructions and moralizing, or who have been reproached and embarrassed for past mistakes. Finally, indecisiveness can result in people who attempt to support more emotionally burdening problems than they can solve. They usually become rattled and can solve none of them.

INFERIOR AND GUILTY

Psychoanalytic literature distinguishes between inferiority feelings and guilt feelings, though both are manifestations of conflict between the actual self and the ideal self. The inner struggle is between what one actually is and what one would like to be, between what one actually does or feels and what one thinks one should do or feel. The fundamental difference is that in *inferiority* feelings, there is a recognition of weakness and inadequacy. People who suffer from inferiority feelings usually provoke competition and aggression. They seek to eradicate their feelings of inferiority by showing their superiority in some form of rivalry. *Guilt* feelings, on the contrary, can be verbalized: "I am not much good. Most of what I want to do (my desires) and have done (my deeds) seem mean and evil. I really deserve contempt and punishment for my failures." Guilt feelings inhibit the competitive spirit. They are reactions to the hostile and aggressive impulses that one feels within the self.

   To get rid of such guilt feelings, we usually try to renounce competition, while inferiority feelings usually invite us to a competitive attitude. Guilt feelings usually persuade us to subordination; they usually surface in self-depreciation and even self-punishment. People generally try to free themselves from inferiority feelings by ambition and competition, by trying to get revenge or the upper hand. The extrication from guilt feelings is usually attempted through submission and the avoidance of any hostile or aggressive behavior. Inferiority feelings tend to produce *rebels;* guilt feelings tend to produce *conformists* with modest and submissive ways.

Ambition and competition remain restricted to the imagination and the phantasy life of guilt-ridden people. They are usually retiring, nonconspicuous types, who assiduously avoid contradictions. They have a tendency to minimize their own abilities. After behaving in a way that their consciences cannot approve, the people with guilt feelings usually resolve that they will never again do the same thing. People with inferiority feelings more often react by asking, "Why not? Why not do these things? I'm not going to give in to external or interior pressures on my conduct!" (See Franz Alexander, *Fundamentals of Psychoanalysis,* 1964.)

INFLAMMABLE—
HANDLE WITH CAUTION

It is hard for most of us to believe this, but people who have "short fuses" and give forth loud noises are frequently reacting to some supposed grievance. But the supposed grievance is not what is really bothering them. As they cannot discuss openly the real source of anger, they are simply letting off steam and their explosions can rarely be taken at face value. What is smoldering in their subconscious is a buried hostility. People are usually much more hostile than they realize. We usually repress our real resentment because our society has conditioned us to believe that hostility is unbecoming in socialized, civilized human beings.

Karl Menninger, in *Love Against Hate*, describes the chain reaction of parents with hidden hostilities frustrating their children and building up in them more repressed hostilities. Then the children grow up into frustrated parents who in turn frustrate themselves and their children. More hostilities! The first step in breaking this chain reaction, Menninger submits, is *to recognize the sources and extent of our aggression and hostility,* of which we are very often unconscious. They are hidden (repressed) because we are led to feel that we can't be angry (especially at our own parents, who have "done so much" for us). After recognizing our true source of hostility, we should try to neutralize these recognized resentments by deepening our understanding or by releasing them in nondestructive ways (athletic competition). It also helps to talk them out. Meanwhile we should be aware that we are often most inflammable with those we love because it is usually against them that we bear the most hostility, since our dealings with them have been longer and more intense.

INTELLECT, THE—
ALIAS THE EGGHEAD

Our social programming often makes it much easier for us to be intellectual and to scorn fuller human reactions, especially insofar as they are emotional. Usually, the role of the "intellect" is assumed by people who are afraid of their emotions or are uncomfortable with them for one reason or another. Perhaps they were programmed not to show them, to think that sentiment was weakness. Sometimes, too, people find themselves unable to relate easily with others, to enjoy friendship, and so they resort to their pose of intellectualism.

The ivory tower of such intellectualism is also a common refuge from the competition involved in human relations. In themselves the learning processes are not as threatening to most of us as are other people. The classroom is preferable to the cold, cruel world we have been taught to fear. More timid souls would rather read about life than try to live. Library stacks can be a retreat from the headaches of daily living, and they can provide the solace of isolation and the prestige of being a scholar. They can also be an escape from social responsibilities.

People programmed for isolation are usually more inclined to scholarly work than to meaningful relations with others. Rather than admit that they are hermits, shut off from society, the players of this game insist that they are dedicated to higher learning. Incidentally, this game frees us from social responsibilities, organizations, committees, paying dues, and making friends. (Please note: This is definitely not intended as an indictment of scholars. The true scholar makes a valuable contribution to society, but no one is called to be a scholar at the expense of being a truly human being, a fully functioning person.)

LONER, THE

There is another escape pattern, or game, which is very much like the ivory tower of intellectualism described above; it is the isolation game. Loners shut themselves off from others, live alone, and try to convince themselves that they like it this way. By entering this kind of solitary confinement, they succeed in evading all the most difficult challenges of human life and society. Loners assume the attitude of smugness; they smirk at organizations, laugh at the poor "joiners," whom they look upon with a pretended attitude of superiority and condescension. They keep telling themselves that they are above this sort of nonsense.

Neurotics are torn between their inner need to push toward and pull away from people. Loners are neurotics who opt in favor of the pulling away from people. They retreat, and since they cannot relate easily to others, they play their game to avoid failures in human relationships. The ultimate effects are conditioned by what is inside of loners, the reasons for their withdrawal tendencies. If it is hostility that is predominant, it could eventually erupt into violence, as with Lee Harvey Oswald. If it is anxiety, it could result in compulsive-obsessive neurotic habits (for example, repeatedly washing hands). If it is paranoia, it will deepen the gulf between themselves and the rest of the human race. The escapist pattern always ends in some kind of lonely tragedy.

MARTYR, THE

The persecution complex (paranoia) of "the martyr" is an emotional disorder characterized by many false suspicious beliefs. Paranoid trends are observed in one kind of schizophrenia, a mental disorder in which the sick person is separated from reality. In neurotic paranoiacs the outstanding characteristic is suspicion. They suffer from what psychologists call "delusions of reference." Such delusions convince paranoiacs that everyone is talking about them, that it rains on the day of their parade because God is holding something against them personally, and so on. It is a feeling of being abused.

It should be said that something of this feeling is in all of us at times; very normal people at times suffer from delusions. In the normal person, however, these delusions are not so irrational, so extreme, or so crippling. Paranoiacs often find themselves in the same predicament as liars, who must invent stories to justify their misrepresentation of the facts. Eventually these delusions become systematized, and paranoid individuals tend to hang on to them in spite of all the apparent inconsistencies.

The persecutory delusions usually grow out of an inferiority complex. Individuals with such delusions hate their own inadequacy and project their thinking into the minds of others; they conclude that others hate them too. They cannot establish satisfactory relationships with others and are generally oversensitive. Their egos are very tender. In feeling rejected by others, they gradually withdraw into themselves and become increasingly estranged and alienated from them. Then they are unable to check their imagined interpretations of the facts that they are misjudging. They feel that they were not suspicious enough of other people, and that others took advantage of them. Now they are too suspicious and feel that they cannot trust anyone.

Normal social relations are impossible to sustain with such an attitude of mind. All of us are somewhat suspicious. The opposite of this normal awareness would be gullibility or naiveté. Paranoiacs have gone much too far. They implement their game by blaming other people for their mistakes. This habit, called "passing the buck," is a normal part of the paranoid delusion. Paranoiacs cannot evaluate properly their own responsibility as distinguishable from the role of others in causing their problems. Their own self-deceptions seem absolutely clear and true to them.

The martyr complex grows out of an unstable self-evaluation and a failure to maintain a satisfactory degree of faith in others. Its expression is to blame others for our unhappiness. Paranoiacs are also aware of their own hostile feelings, but rationalize them with their delusions. Their desire is to attack others because they feel persecuted. Delusions in this way are simply attempts to create an imaginary situation in which the symptoms experienced within can appear rational and acceptable. Paranoiacs' capacity for rationalization is often remarkable, and sometimes they succeed in convincing others of the rationality of their behavior.

MESSIAH, THE

This game calls for a little imagination (and a subconscious need to feel important). Messiahs fancy themselves saviors of the human race. It could well be a reaction formation to the fear of insignificance. They think of themselves as the "helper" and others as the "helped" in almost all of their relationships. Instead of urging others to use their own strength and wisdom, messiahs dutifully lend out theirs. They relate to very few people as equals. If people are attracted to messiahs because of their good qualities that are not completely submerged by their assumed role, it will be easier for these people if they have a problem or need. It will be an admission ticket.

The gain of the game is a rather large, expansive feeling and a long, well-memorized list of those who have been helped. Basically, messiahs have inferiority feelings and seek to free themselves from these by dominating others emotionally.

When I repress my emotions,
my stomach keeps score.

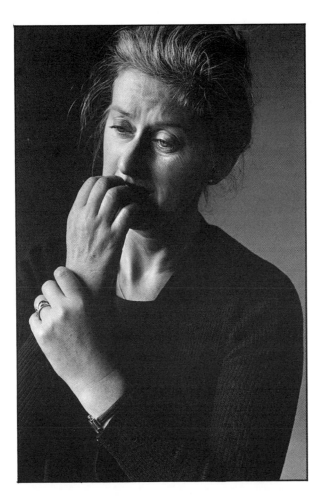

MOMMY, THE

The overprotective mother (or, more rarely, a father) plays a very harmful game. Mommies usually produce little monsters, utterly selfish people who demand their own way in every-thing. Such children are tragically unprepared for a world that is simply unwilling to baby them and accede to their every whim. Psychological studies done on soldiers in wartime show that those who "crack up" most often and most severely are the products of overprotective mothers. The most often requested song of soldiers, when Bing Crosby visited the South Pacific troops in World War II, was Brahm's "Lullaby."

  This game is not motivated by a genuine, healthy, and mature love. There are three possible causes: (1) *Neurotic anxiety.* The insecure mother is fearful that her children may suffer some harm unless she does everything for them. This fear is usually transmitted to her children. Such a mother does not enjoy her children and only worries about them. (2) *Hostility.* Strange as this may seem, maternal overprotection is sometimes an overcompensation (reaction formation) for a subconscious hostility toward her children. She atones for her personal dislike of her children by conscientious devotion to them. (3) *Frustrated marital relations.* The mother who is unhappy with her husband frequently pours her pent-up feelings of affection on her children. Under such circumstances the children bear the brunt of the unsatisfied love life of the mother. (See David Levy, *Maternal Overprotection* [Columbia University Press, 1966].)

PEACE AT ANY PRICE

(See "Inferior and Guilty.")

PONCE DE LEON

This is the game of people who are aging and simply cannot adjust to the fact. Frequently, middle-aged people feel that they are losing their physical attractiveness. Baldness, the middle-age spread, wrinkles around the neck—all symbolize declining prestige among the opposite sex. To compensate for this deterioration of age, those who have never developed as true persons and who have never developed deeper emotional ties with others usually begin looking for a young lover. In addition to the physical evidence, which shows in the mirror, these people also compensate for an emotional "slump," which is evidenced in loss of ambition, fatigue, and more frequent fits of depression. Biologically, this can be due to insufficient hormone production.

The tragedy of this game is that these people have suffered emotional arrest and have never learned to relate meaningfully as persons; they have very little left for consolation in middle age. They have prized their "sex appeal" and fear that it is waning. Sadly, they try to hide their double chins, varicose veins, the wrinkles, gray hair, and so on. They keep trying to think and act young. Sex appeal has never been and could never be the key to the finer things in life. It certainly does not sustain us in the process of aging.

POOR MOUTH, THE

This game is played by those who appear to be self-depreciating. The players talk themselves down, perhaps in search of reassurances that assuage their "guilt feelings." (See also "Inferior and Guilty.")

POUTER, THE

The pouting game is played by emotional children. Pouters cannot sit down and openly discuss interpersonal problems, usually because their position or grievance is irrational and they secretly know it. They can scourge others emotionally by their silence, sad looks, and so on, without having to tell these people what is bothering them. They can sulk without accepting the responsibility of having to explain why they are acting this way. A full explanation might sound so silly that they know (peripherally) that the other person might even laugh. However, they can derive their needed satisfaction and indulge their own self-pity without having to work out difficult situations through communication. (See also "Fragile—Handle with Care.")

PREJUDICE AND BIGOTRY

This game is the outgrowth of a social neurosis that flourishes chiefly among the insecure. Prejudiced people need some kind of vent for their emotional hostilities. The personal development of the chosen scapegoat in this situation will certainly not be helped if he or she is abused in this way. Gordon Allport, in *The Nature of Prejudice,* suggests that prejudice arises from our anxieties. We feel insecure, and so we form around us an in-group as a kind of buffer of protection. Those outside of my in-group are thought to be a threat and menace. I lash out at them because I am somehow threatened by them. I cannot logically suggest why (though many reasons are adduced), but anyone who is not in my in-group is necessarily a threat to me if I am highly anxious and insecure.

Prejudice is an emotional delusion. Still, wherever it exists, it is never recognized as such by those who are afflicted by it. Bigots will inevitably try to explain their prejudice in intellectual terms. They could hardly admit the irrationality of their position. But the very term *prejudice* means a premature judgment, a judgment made before all the evidence is considered.

Society very often helps us with the work of the rationalization needed to explain our prejudices;

most bigots therefore don't have to work out their own rationalized, logical explanations. They can just recite well-rehearsed lines.

PROCRASTINATOR, THE

The "mañana" game attempts to evade reality by postponing the things that should be done—that should be done here and now. Procrastinators have to deceive themselves by unrealistic assurances, like, "I'll cut down on my smoking as soon as I can go on a vacation." "I'll start exercising when the weather gets better." "I'll start going to church again when I settle down and have my own family and children." Escaping into vague and unrealistic tomorrows is only one of the many varieties of evasion of reality that we commonly seek. (See "Indecisive and Uncertain.")

RESENTFULLY YOURS

When born-loser types look for a scapegoat for their own failure, they very often blame someone or something else: the establishment, life, the breaks. They resent the success and happiness of others because their own lives, by comparison, are unhappy. They have been somehow deprived. We are all tempted to make our own failures understandable by explaining them in terms of something other than our own inade-quacies. Unfair treatment by others, injustice, the conspiracy of circumstances, and so on, make it easier for us to face our failures.

Resenters use up all their energies resenting, and therefore they usually accomplish very little. Sometimes it seems that the most vicious critics of anything (national government, school, church) are very often the ones that do nothing for the institutions they criticize so vocally. Resentful people are forever trying to bring their case before the court of life, hoping that the jury of others will acquit them of their failures.

Resentment comes from the Latin *resentire* ("to feel all over again"). Resenters are always rehearsing and rehashing the past. They insist on reliving past battles they cannot win, and they often persist in this game for a lifetime. Resent-ment becomes an emotional habit. No one's feelings are caused by others. Our feelings are caused by our own emotional response, our own choices and reactions. Resenters are reactors, not actors, and eventually, when they realize this, they are left with no vestiges of self-respect. They have spent their lives employing a failure mechanism, and they somehow know it. Resentment is a cop-out.

SEX BOMB AND
PREDATORY MALE, THE

Barring the sick condition of the nymphomaniac who is obsessed with sex, most girls who play the "sex bomb" game do so not because they really enjoy genital sexuality or because they are "highly sexed." It is rather because they feel they have nothing else to offer but a provocative body. They want to gain male attention, and they desire to be popular. The ruse of this game usually pays off, but the emotionally arrested males it attracts are always very regrettable conquests. Besides this sad motive of reaching out for affection and attention, sometimes the "sex bomb" is trying to reject her parents, to spite them.

"The predatory male" is usually an ego-hunter, looking for some new trophy of conquest. His inferiority feelings (see "Inferior and Guilty") are deep, and he wants to compensate for them by trying to make conquests of the opposite sex. Sometimes, successful "ladies' men" are merely neurotics who are industriously engaged in an attempt to cover up their personal insecurity. They are more to be pitied than censored.

The sadness of both "sex bomb" and "predatory male" is that they are seeking some kind of human intimacy or nearness. Because personal closeness takes a long time and

demands much honesty (gut-level communication), and because these people feel totally
inadequate to pay this price of true personal
intimacy, they substitute physical for personal
intimacy. They are not equipped, they feel, to do
any better. People are not attracted to the useless
side of life, Alfred Adler says in his book *What
Life Should Mean to You*, unless they fear that they
will be defeated if they remain on the useful side.
Those who play this game are usually so
emotionally undeveloped that the Don Juan
pattern claims them for life. They are unable to
confer their love lastingly on anyone, if, indeed,
they are capable of love at all.

STRONG, SILENT TYPE, THE,
VS. WILLING AND WORDY

There are two ways to keep from communicating yourself to others, and because of various fears, most of us are reluctant to let others know who we really are. The two very effective techniques to prevent communication are (1) to say very little. People may think that you are profound if you don't open your mouth. An old saw says that "still waters run deep." The other way is (2) to say so much that no one can possibly sort it all out and figure out anything about you. You can't say a great deal, using this buckshot technique of obscurity, without giving a lot of contradictory indications. No one can possibly accuse you of not doing your part to communicate. Only the sharper members of the group will realize that they don't know what the devil you've been talking about.

SUFFERING IS THE
SPICE (PRICE) OF LIFE

Some neurotics have been so conditioned that they feel guilty for enjoying anything in life. As Abraham Lincoln once said, "People are about as happy as they decide that they are going to be." This masochistic game calls for renewed penance for every pleasure. These people rarely spend money on frivolous things; they do not really enjoy an evening if the price of admission is high. They tend to get involved in love situations that are hopeless and become infatuated by someone who is totally beyond their reach. If they do catch themselves having a good time, they will devise, like a contrite sinner, some manner of punishing themselves for it. Material gains seem futile and meaningless, and such sufferers rarely realize that the deficiency is really inside themselves.

Fundamentally, the problem is often buried guilt feelings. These people don't think that they deserve to have pleasant thoughts or to enjoy good times. People who are programmed for this game tend to paranoia. They project their self-hatred into others, believing that others must feel about them as they themselves do. Such people are also very concerned to please others and dread disapproval. They are not able to relate deeply to many people, if any at all, because their basic self-hatred sabotages all their relationships.

WORRIER, THE

Rollo May, in his book *The Meaning of Anxiety*, says that normal anxiety is proportioned to the objective threat or danger to the existence of an individual as a person. Neurotic anxiety, however, is *disproportionate* to the objective danger. The most common cause of disproportionate anxiety is the insecurity an individual has experienced as an infant and child. If infants are not given the needed sensations of security—if they are not held in secure arms, rocked tenderly to sleep, and so on—and if children are not sure of their parents' love, their level of anxiety will probably be high. The game always follows the program.

As a game, worry is an immature way to handle difficulties. Worriers usually get on a treadmill, go over the same ground again and again, getting nowhere. (In the end, however, they get ulcers.) They repeat useless statements of their problem, rehearse alternatives without reaching any decision. They calculate all the possible consequences of possible decisions again and again. Worriers would probably feel guilty for not doing anything constructive, so they do something: they worry. (Got a term paper coming up?)

Psychologically, worry is related to anxiety, which results from supercharged *repressed (hidden) emotions* (for example, hostility) with or without any external threats. It is therefore possible for chronic worriers to feel ill at ease without knowing what is actually bothering them. The internal pressures of repressed emotions do not always need external stimuli to produce this uncomfortable feeling. It is one of the high prices we pay for emotional repression.

"Sorry,
but that is the way I am...
I was like this in the beginning,
am now, and ever shall be..."
is a handy motto and delusion
to have around you if you
don't want to grow up.